ACQUIRING OUR IMAGE OF GOD

ACQUIRING OUR IMAGE
OF GOD

The Emotional Basis
for Religious Education

Martin A. Lang

PAULIST PRESS ● NEW YORK/RAMSEY

Library of Congress
Catalog Card Number: 82-62968

ISBN: 0-8091-2537-4

Published by Paulist Press
545 Island Road, Ramsey, N.J. 07446

Printed and bound in the
United States of America

CONTENTS

To My Son
Jay

FOREWORD

Religious education in the various Christian churches has undergone considerable change within a single generation. It is now clear that such education must involve far more than the cognitive, and that even this cognitive component must be communicated in ways very different from the traditional set of rational propositions. In his present work Martin Lang focuses upon the emotional component of the faith experience. He does so with care and imagination, and with the resources that only someone of his wide professional experience can command. Syntheses of this kind are a distinct service to both parents and religious educators, both of whom are in constant need of new insights and guidance in their difficult task of handing on the faith.

Dr. Lang's contribution is distinctive by reason of his emphasis throughout upon the connection between meaning systems and what he terms "bonding." The religious story-myths which give structure to Christian lives not only tell us our place in the universe but also our proper relationships, our "bondings," to God and to each other. Such story-myths appeal to our emotions at their deepest level, and this is what constitutes both their strength and their danger. I am reminded of what Mark Twain once said: religion is pretty dangerous stuff if you get it wrong. Lang's concern is that religious educators not focus attention exclusively upon the "relevance" aspect of these story-myths of faith, but rather inquire into their "bonding" aspect, that is to say, into whether a given story-myth correlates with the needs, hopes and expectations of a given person, generated by his or her history of interpersonal relationships.

Within this overall intent Martin Lang explores the phenomenon

1

of religious growth from childhood through the teens to adulthood. He shows that at each stage bonding is the bearer of meaning. It ties us to our tradition emotionally, even as our reason grapples at various stages with those difficulties inherent in all religious stories. His chapters on integration are especially helpful in seeing this experience as the turning point in one's religious life-experience, in which we gain a sense of our true selves and our true relationship as individuals to God. He argues that in the future this inner pilgrimage of growth must receive greater attention from religious educators. For without such attention they cannot assist persons to see in events the primary locus of God's activity in their lives, nor can they help persons connect their personal stories with the communal story of the Christian community as a whole. Lang's final chapter on practical applications draws upon his years in the classroom and upon his work as a guidance counselor, and it should prove valuable indeed. His book as a whole augurs well that changing emphases in religious education will continue to advantage both the churches and their membership.

Christopher F. Mooney, S. J.

PREFACE

There is something very satisfying about being a parent—and something very disturbing. What is satisfying is sharing in the unfolding growth of another life which we have helped bring into this world. What is disturbing is watching significant aspects of that same growth take place entirely apart from our influence. To a parent, the nature-nurture issue is far more than a speculative question. It is an ongoing, involving family matter.

The practical implications of the nature-nurture controversy are of particularly vital concern where religious faith is at stake. Parents who care deeply about the lives of their children want them to grow up treasuring the same faith that they have come to appreciate in their own lives. Sometimes they are disappointed in this expectation in spite of what they consider their best efforts. At other times they are surprised and amazed at the growth of faith beyond their expectations.

The problem remains: what kind of impact do parents make on the religious ideas and values of their children? Are they really able to share the most basic insights and convictions of their religious lives? Is it possible to determine anything significant about faith sharing, not only between parent and child but between other human beings who care deeply for each other?

These are the questions, fundamental to religious education, which have intrigued me for many years. They are the questions, I have discovered, that intrigue many others as well. Not only are people anxious to discover how they can help their children grow, but they are also deeply curious about their own growth and why they think and feel the way they do in matters religious.

3

That is why, I think, I have received such enthusiastic help from the many people who agreed to be interviewed. They are the first ones I wish to thank for their generous and frank cooperation in sharing some of their most personal thoughts with me. Each contributed at least four hours to these interviews; some contributed much more time. Graduate students in Religious Education at Fairfield University, who worked with me, also interviewed a large number of subjects; the results of their efforts also are incorporated into this study. The thesis of Sr. Irene Comeau, S.S.J., was especially helpful in contributing children's images of God.

I am indebted to Mr. Joseph Cunneen, editor of *Cross Currents*, for his very helpful comments at an early stage of the manuscript and to Sidney Callahan for her encouraging conversations while the main ideas were being drafted. I am grateful also to Fr. Christopher Mooney, S.J., for his kind reading and helpful comments as well as for his generous writing of the Foreword. Toward the end of the literary journey Msgr. Robert Fuller, of Renew, was very encouraging in seeing connections between this work and the process of parish renewal, in which he is a leader.

Fairfield University contributed greatly by granting a sabbatical semester during which I was able to polish the final drafts of the manuscript. In the typing, my secretary, Mrs. Kathleen Clark, was, as ever, of invaluable assistance. Finally, no acknowledgement is sufficient for the support and sheer endurance of my wife, Carol Anne, who with our children, suffered my absence patiently as this manuscript went through its many "final" drafts.

RELIGION AND LIFE MEANING

Chapter One

On a gorgeous May morning at the ocean's edge, when the sun finally began to show some real warmth and a crisp freshness filled the air, even Coney Island seemed to share a touch of paradise. It was a Sunday in 1981 and a small religious group stood together singing and praying, their flowing white garments lapping in the cool breeze.

A semicircular ring of curious onlookers stood a few yards behind them, interested not only in the worshipers but in the TV news cameras as well. At a still further distance, but unmistakenly present to the scene, the famous chestnut horses of the New York City mounted police pawed impatiently in the sand, the blue helmets of their riders intensified by the clear blue morning sky.

Rumor had it that some members of the sect would plunge to their deaths in the chilling ocean waters, walking out into the waves to meet their expected Lord.

Impatient for action, a TV newscaster finally asked one of the leaders whether anybody was going to jump in. The ambiguous answer—that the group believed in life, not death—kept the cameras rolling as the worshipers, seemingly unaware of the commotion around them, went about the rituals of their morning service.

Nobody died, but the police were there and the media were there because three years earlier a mass suicide in Guyana indelibly impressed its lesson on the modern mind. Religion can have an enormous influence over human life. It leads people to do anything, leave home, family, country, even give up their lives, as in Guyana, as a sacrifice for what they believe in.

In the mass suicide in Guyana all of the participants, surely, were not depressed, nor were they insane. Hours earlier they had no intention of giving up their lives. Yet, when the moment came, their suicidal act, understood perhaps as a final symbol of total dedication, seemed incipiently credible, seemed somehow to fit into what had become their total "meaning system."

The meaning system that the Rev. Jim Jones proposed called for a brotherhood of blacks and whites in a single community. It led them to flee the structures of an established society and start fresh in the unspoiled jungles of Guyana.

The Mormons, a century earlier, chose to live out their vision of reality amid the desolate hills overlooking the Great Salt Lake. A new vision of reality often requires preliminary isolation, if only to get as far away as possible from persecutors. The early Christians did the same thing in the catacombs and the Puritans did it by moving to the new world.

The Rev. Jim Jones obviously had a life-and-death grip on his followers, and this, too, is characteristic of religious commitment. Countless numbers of people throughout history have readily given their lives, and give them today, for their religious beliefs.

Gordon Allport, the late Harvard psychologist, thought that meaning systems that were rooted in religious values and attitudes were the most comprehensive in people's lives, not only governing life and death but giving rationales for suffering and poverty, for accidents and human weakness, explaining man in the universe and offering the hope of an afterlife.[1]

It would be a mistake, though, to think of "meaning systems" as if they were highly rational philosophies of life. Religion is by no means a purely intellectual process. In fact, a religious meaning system can tolerate a host of intellectual incongruities if it has a strong central thrust that touches the core of a person's being.

The insanity of ending one's own life and the lives of one's children is surely the height of incongruity in the Jones' cult which was established on the principle of caring for each other and seeking a better life together. But human sacrifice has not been unknown to religion when it is set into a rationale that makes it appear proper at the time.

Ancient peoples, from the Canaanites of the Middle East to the Aztecs of Mexico, found appropriate conditions for the sacrifice of human life.

This irrational conduct is always set into the framework of a larger story which appeals to its adherents in several ways but strongly at the emotional level. The Jones' cult, for example, proposed a certain vision of humankind in which deep human relationships between the races were possible. Most found themselves bound to one another and to their founder by warm emotional bonds.

Deep Emotions Essential
to Meaning Systems

The emotional, passionate elements are essential to religious meaning systems. The religious devotee has to love someone. The particular story of each religious group is a story of bonding—bonding to God, bonding to the founder, bonding to one's fellow human beings. Bonding negates the aloneness of people and situates them in a society where they feel they belong.

It is the passionate bonding that carries religiously committed persons willingly into the area of the intellectually incongruous. It may also carry them into what many others would call the patently immoral. The theologian Reinhold Niebuhr saw this force operating both for good and for evil in society: "The greater the vitality of religion, the more it may either support or endanger morality. It may create moral sensitivity and destroy moral vigor by the force of the same vitality."[2]

The vitality enters into meaning systems by stories, examples, models rather than by philosophical treatises. The parables of Jesus have touched the hearts of men and moved them to commitment for twenty centuries. The power of the rabbis to reach their people lay in the many colorful stories they told, taken from both Scripture and legend to dramatize lessons about justice and truth.

There are stories that tell of human origins and of the origins of a particular religious group. There are stories that concretize the ideals of the group and stories that show how the ideals are corrupted. There are stories about the heroes and about the failures. All of these propose real life models whose conduct should be imitated or avoided.

Not *every* story has deeply gripping emotional content. Take, for example, the very basic creation stories of the Judaeo-Christian tradition. They carry solid foundations of meaning even for many people who never go near a church or synagogue. They are stories they heard in childhood that say there is Someone in control of what is happening. There is a purpose to being on earth. That is reassuring and can find easy acceptance into a meaning system, particularly in childhood.

The bonding element may not be too strong in the stories but it is present. It says that man belongs to God. It positions him in the universe. The creation stories provide a context in which there is a place for man to fit in. Any story that makes a contribution to a meaning system will have some bonding content to it. And, of course, within every religious tradition there are stories that are deeper bonders than others.

The creation stories clearly set the pattern that God is in charge of this world. Certainly, in Judaism as in Christianity, God is the maker of history; his hand is intimately involved in the course of human affairs.

Additionally, in the stories about the prophets and throughout the Torah itself God is eminently a God of justice, the One who cares for the deprived, is concerned for widows and orphans. He punishes injustice. He rewards mercy.

But what happens when the experiences of life call into question the truth of these fundamental beliefs? Or, put another way, what happens when the pillars of a meaning system are catastrophically shaken? There are two clear alternatives: either the meaning system holds or it collapses hopelessly under the strain.

There is a story told by survivors of a Nazi death camp of a group of rabbis conducting a very serious trial of God's actions in the holocaust. They investigated every reason that might be adduced to justify his conduct. Every night in their barracks, even though they were exhausted by their day's work, they met to discuss the evidence. What purpose or reason could God have for permitting the innocent, infants and children, to be punished so severely? What sins, what infidelities could warrant such judgments?

When all was fully discussed, when every conceivable argument was produced in God's behalf, it was time to turn in a final verdict. With deep sorrow in their hearts they arrived at their decision: God must be judged guilty. He had punished his people beyond the bounds of justice. The God of justice had transgressed justice!

In less dire circumstances this would have been an unpardonable blasphemy. Here it was the last ditch stand of a meaning system. One of the pillars did not come down. It held tenaciously under the strain: God was still in charge, albeit acting unjustly. No one could say why God was doing what he did but God was still God. He was in charge in human affairs.

In this example the rational aspects of the meaning system were thrown into shambles. The rabbis clung desperately to the bonding that joined them to their God. At other times, in other circumstances, with other examples in history the rational elements of their belief system could be verified. But under these conditions only the tenuous strands of an earlier bonding still held them to their God.

Abraham Heschel expressed this same kind of unswerving faith when he reflected on the holocaust in the light of Psalm 44:

> All this has come upon us,
> Though we have not forgotten Thee,
> Or been false to Thy covenant.
> Our heart has not turned back.
> Nor have our steps departed from Thy way. . . .
> . . . for Thy sake we are slain. . . .
> Why dost Thou hide Thy face?[3]

Unlike the rabbis and unlike Heschel it was the man who was totally unable to classify what was happening to him who was defenseless. Stripped of the rationalities of human experience and also stripped of the emotional commitments of religious purposes he stood naked in his torment. All bonds had been broken. Life had become essentially meaningless.

For those victims of the holocaust who let go of the main pillars of their meaning system there was nothing left, no reason for suffering, not even a God to question. As Viktor Frankl tells us, they accepted death as a welcome end to meaningless suffering.[4]

The Story Informs the Meaning System

The structure of a meaning system is not usually a tightly bricked edifice. It does not have an explanation for every eventuality or even for most eventualities. But it does establish a fundamental perception of what is happening in human life. This fundamental perception is most frequently communicated through a series of stories. Many scholars call the stories that help to structure reality for people "myths."

There are two general understandings of myth in our society today and the meanings attached to each are quite different.[5] One is the popular understanding that says a myth is something that a lot of people believe but is really not true. For example, it is a myth that eating a lot of sweets causes acne in teenagers. In this understanding myths are deceptions. They need to be exploded. There is no such thing as a useful myth. It is simply bad information.

The other understanding is the one that enjoys popularity in the scholarly worlds of anthropology, literature, philosophy and religion. Myths are stories that help to explain the condition of man in his world. These mythical stories give a structure and a meaning to reality that man can readily understand. In the mythical story man sees himself explained, he sees his proper relationship to God or the gods, he learns what is proper bonding, where his place is in the universe. Myths set up the parameters of the meaning system. Therefore myths are not to be discarded. They are extremely important and they are *true*.

When I say they are true I mean that they convey a real truth about man to the hearer. They are the vehicles for communicating something very true and very worthwhile in human life.

The Story Has a "Now" Meaning

For ancient man myths about the beginnings of the world, about the origins of fire or about the forces of evil helped to provide a way of thinking. This way of thinking about the world then helped him to cope with the problems and joys of living. The myths helped to shape his meaning system.

Since the ancient myths have no current applications to modern life they appear in the popular imagination as the fantastic escapades of sky gods, winged creatures or unicorns that make no sense at all.

They have no current application. That is an important point. When a myth loses its currency or what I call its "now" character it loses its meaning. It fails in its task of clarifying one or other aspect of human life.

Our present day meaning systems are still informed by myths but we usually do not think of them in those terms. We have, for example, a very nice myth about Thanksgiving that helps to contribute to our meaning system as "Americans." It is not the kind of life-and-death myth with its serious implications that make up religious meaning systems but it does help us to perceive what we mean when we say we are "Americans." The myth conveys very real meanings all right, and the country would miss Thanksgiving if it were taken away. Let us take a closer look at it for a moment.

In the month of November the newspapers begin to break out the supermarket ads for turkeys, the school children repaper their classroom walls with Pilgrims and Indians. Suburban and city kindergarteners grind out mounds of cranberry relish for their admiring parents. The national consciousness gears up for an eating feast.

The myth tells the story of the first settlers who risked everything for their freedom, for a better life. The children, grandchildren and great-grandchildren of Irish, Italian, German, Greek, Japanese immigrants (and all the others) identify with the story—and for a very good reason. It is their story, too. It is the story of their own family coming to America. The latest boat people from Vietnam can understand it.

The reward for the courage to leave everything else behind is a better way of living, the blessings of abundance, a new feeling of freedom.

The Pilgrims and the Indians make a colorful story. They provide the mythical story content that bristles with meaning. They give the rational base for celebrating the joy of being in this country. But to go into it too deeply intellectually is to ruin it. Simply pass the white meat and dig in! It is a perfect holiday for a bleak month.

So goes the myth. It is one way Americans have of celebrating their identity. There are many other myths that help us look upon ourselves positively. When we hear them we forget about people burning our flags in foreign countries, deriding pictures of our presidents and killing our ambassadors. For example, when we tell our children about Abraham Lincoln we talk of a boy raised in the backwoods who through hard work educated himself and became the president of the United States. He did not claw his way to a better life, to power and influence. He worked for it.

The myth says that ordinary people can rise to power and wealth in the land where all are born equal. Rock stars, country-western singers and big time athletes become rich and influential overnight before our eyes, bearing witness to the truth of the myth.

That is an important dimension of the myth, its current application, or, as I have called it, its "now" character. The myth helps *present* understandings. As people celebrate Thanksgiving they are grateful that they can put that amount of food on the table *now*. A myth is dead if it has no contemporary meaning.

In spite of the discrepancy between the popular and the scholarly meaning of the word "myth" the academic community continues to use myth in the ways in which I have described. This is true in the many fields connected with studies in the humanities.

The Foundation Story as a Focal Point of Meaning

Some scholars in the field of religious studies do not hesitate to use the word myth to describe stories about the Hebrew patriarchs, about Moses and about Christ. They might speak of the creation myth, for example, or a Church foundation myth.

The late Norman Perrin, a distinguished New Testament scholar, describes the final scene in St. Matthew's Gospel as a foundation myth. Let us see what he means.[6]

Just before his ascension into heaven Jesus gives his final address to the disciples gathered before him: "Go forth therefore and make all nations my disciples; baptize men everywhere in the name of the Father and the Son and the Holy Spirit and teach them to observe all that I have commanded you" (Mt 28:19-20—New English Bible).

The scene is strongly visual in character. We can picture the eleven gathered around Jesus listening intently to his very last words. They are more significant than even his words on the cross.

The words are spoken directly to the listener by Christ. What must the disciple do? Christ tells him, "Make disciples of all nations." Show people how to live out his challenging teachings. The "now" character of the story is evident. It has been understood clearly by every succeeding generation of Christians. The point is to spread the teachings of Christ and baptize others, that is, affiliate them. The message is addressed directly to the hearer.

Then there is the bonding, the emotional content. The baptizing is the affiliating, the relating. As the disciple is affiliated, related to Christ, so he must invite others to affiliate themselves. The final words of the passage and of the entire Gospel cement the affiliation: "And be assured, I am with you always, to the end of time."

The scene is a summation of what the whole previous Gospel has said. It enjoins the hearer to follow Christ and to urge others to do the same. Baptism is the basic symbol of this following. The Christian Church can point to this scene for its charter. It can say, "Look, this is exactly what we are doing when we invite others to faith. We are clearly following out the final and most important words of our founder." That is a foundation myth. Any church that leaves out baptism, does not instruct in the teachings of Christ and does not make converts lacks the minimum essentials for being called Christian.

This religious story, if appropriated by the listener, can become a point of self-identification. What does it mean to be a Christian? It means to do what was said in this scene. So we have a structural component in one's meaning system. Just as Thanksgiving has a part in telling people about their American heritage, so this scene has a part in telling them about their Christian heritage.

What scene in the Hebrew Scriptures tells Jews of their heritage? What is a foundation myth for Judaism? It is the story of the exodus celebrated at Passover. In the exodus God performed the paradigmatic act of freeing his people from slavery and oppression. Every Jewish child knows the story. It is an age-old story still being re-enacted today. God is the liberator while humankind is the oppressor. For a people, often enslaved by others and still, in many parts of the world, stripped of full religious liberty, it is a perenially fresh call to liberation.

To think of oneself as Jewish is to know the threat of possible or real oppression and discrimination. So the story lives and speaks to many people today. People who are different in color, in nationality, in culture can find a common bond in a foundation myth which unites them in their faith and helps establish their identity.

Stories that have a celebrative, festive character imprint themselves most deeply upon our meaning systems. For example, we have just spoken of the exodus and Passover. Passover is a home feast and a table feast. If a Jewish family lets go of this celebration in their own home or with relatives they are letting go of their identity as Jews. By the same token Christians who do not have a child baptized are letting

go of their self-identification as Christians. The here-and-now celebra-
tions that are connected with stories help to embed these stories in the
consciousness. What could be embedded more deeply than the celebration of Christmas for a five year old? The toys, the decorations, the
food, all enhance the story-myth immeasurably.

The telling of the stories (which you may or may not want to call
myths) along with the joyous or even sorrowful commemoration of
them in feasts helps to set up the structural elements in people's meaning systems. Before we are old enough to know what is happening we
are being socialized into the myths and feasts of our religion and our
cultural heritage.

Three Distinctive Aspects
of the Religious Story

There are three aspects to a story-myth that make it a powerful
vehicle for transmitting meaning. The first aspect is its emotional content. It is the appeal in the story that is made to our feelings. The strong
story makes us cry or laugh or feel depressed or elated. It moves us.

In the life of Jesus we are presented with many moving stories.
The newborn infant, beautiful and cuddly, has no place to stay. We
picture him being among the animals in a stable and we realize who
he is. Then we see him as a young man helping everyone who comes
to him. His heart goes out to every sick person, every widow, every
child. He is moved to tears in the presence of suffering and death. In
the end this gentle, loving man is tortured, brutalized and murdered.
He dies with forgiveness on his lips. For centuries this story and the
sub-stories within it have inspired millions of people. If they did not
have emotional appeal they would not speak to the total person.

There is another dimension to the emotional content in the strong
religious story. It is what I call the bonding. The difference between
believers and unbelievers hearing the same story about the life of Jesus
lies in the affiliation that proceeds from it. The believers *feel* related
to Jesus. They appropriate the religious story into their own story so
that, for example, Jesus becomes their Savior.

The non-believers hear a moving story about a man who lived two
thousand years ago but do not close the gap between the historical personality and themselves. They do not feel related to Jesus. The two

stand in separate zones, isolated from each other. The zone in which the self resides must fuse into the zone of the story-myth so that the self can say, "It is for me; it is about me; it is mine," if it will appropriate the story into its meaning system. Bonding is a matter of feeling. People are not bonded unless they feel bonded. They are bonded when they feel emotionally related.

That brings us to the second aspect of the strong religious story-myth, its "now" character. We have seen that unless a story-myth has meaning right "now" it will not have the power to exert influence. It has to aid our present understanding of the world, of others and of ourselves. But as we have labored to say, this understanding is not divorced from bonding. The "now" character of a religious story is not an isolated "moral" or a principle to be learned. It comes clothed in feeling.

To help clarify this let us imagine two people reading the Sermon on the Mount from differing perspectives. One reads it as an interesting historical literary piece written halfway through the first century. In so doing one might compare it with something in the Hebrew Scriptures. One's thoughts might run along these lines: "The Beatitudes seem to be built on Psalm 119. And the three Jewish ascetical practices are mentioned—prayer, fasting and almsgiving—but they're put differently. I wonder whether Jesus originally made these connections or whether it was the work of the evangelist." Or others might read the injunctions about turning the other cheek and loving one's enemies and then say to themselves: "This is a very demanding level of morality. Most people don't seem to be able to measure up to it." They might be glad that they read the text directly (perhaps for a college assignment) because it gave them a clear picture of what the early Christian ideals were all about.

In this reading, the text of the Sermon is not for them now. They do not feel emotionally related to it. They stand apart from it and look at it as an historical document. No appropriation is considered and none occurs.

In a different reading of the same text, believers who feel "related" to Jesus hear the sermon addressed to them personally. It is as if they were sitting at the feet of Jesus and listening to what they must do if they wish to be faithful followers. The injunctions about turning the other cheek and loving one's enemies challenge them to try harder. They feel called to observe prayer, fasting and almsgiving in the spirit in which the Master has explained it. If Jesus taught this two thousand years ago, that does not matter. The sermon is Christ's word now which bypasses time and contemporizes the teaching. Each word is addressed to them in their uniqueness. That constitutes a religious reading of the text.

I have explained two aspects of the strong religious story-myth. It seems obvious in these, the emotional element and the "now" character, that the believers are the *emotionally receptive* ones. They are predisposed to accept the story. They come to it expecting it to be their story. In theological terms we would say that they come to it with faith although we do not want to simply equate faith with feeling. Feeling is contained in faith.

For the non-believers the story, right from the beginning, is not their own. It stands apart from them, to be dipped into, to be assessed but not to be appropriated. When Mohandas Gandhi first read the Sermon on the Mount he was impressed. He did not, however, accept the content as his own. He did not become a disciple of Jesus. He incorporated some of the teachings into his own meaning system, remaining a Hindu who had been enriched by this material.

The fundamental orientation that we have when we come to a story-myth helps to determine to what degree we will absorb its message. This is an important part of the study of life meaning systems and we will return to it again a little later.

The third aspect of the strong religious story which we have not emphasized yet is its visual character. By that I mean that it can be pictured vividly and concretely in the imagination. We have seen how the foundation myth of the ascension can be remembered with all of the disciples gathered around and Jesus telling them his last wishes. We can picture the scene and are thereby focused to be receptive to the message of the story-myth.

The crucifixion is another powerful example. Since the Renaissance it has been depicted by artists in a variety of ways. Each piece of artwork intends to evoke certain emotions and each invites our participation. So in a similar way each reader of the passion of Jesus draws his or her own mental image of the scene which serves as a baseline for thoughts and emotions connected with the story.

Every good story-myth has a visual dimension to it that serves as an attention base. It rivets interest so that the listeners are prepared to invest themselves emotionally and hear the full import of the message. We each paint our own mental image out of the select materials of our own imagination.

There are therefore three aspects to the strong religious story-myth: (1) the emotional content with its possibility for bonding, (2) the "now" character which supplies contemporary meaning, and (3) the visual dimension which serves as a focus for the imagination. These three elements are intimately related in each story. When people come to a story-myth with the appropriate subjective conditions it is possible that they will incorporate the perspective of that story-myth into their total life meaning system.

Unchanging Character of Biblical Stories

In the Judaeo-Christian body of Scripture *all* of the story-myths are "unchanging." They have been permanently fixed long ago. No one can add a new story about Abraham or a parable of Jesus that has not been heard before. Jews and Christians read the same stories over and over again at their services of worship, and this has been going on for centuries.

If these stories are to remain religious readings, enormously moving, and not simply historical curiosities, they must appeal to each generation, say something that can be appropriated by people who live at very different times in history. They must maintain their "now" meaning.

Each of us enters history within a certain life context. It is this context that governs the "now" application of the story-myths that we learn. The people of each historical period and even of each different culture understand the story-myths of their faith in the idioms of their own time. The understanding of a basic story is a derivative of the world-view that is prevalent at a certain time. Just from the point of view of language and its reflection of cultural understandings, translating the Bible is an ongoing generational task.

To put it another way, the stories do not change but the people do, from one generation to the next. If the stories are going to continue to appeal they must have a "now" application that can make a contribution to the meaning system of people who live at this time in history.

Young men in the thirteenth century who studied at the University of Paris with their fascinating teacher Thomas Aquinas would gladly get up in the morning, perhaps even after a night of beering, in order to hear him integrate the teachings of the then popular Arab philosophers with the ancient Greeks and make it all coalesce with the Christian faith. They could deal with creation in philosophical terms. But they did not have to cope with the findings of Newton or Kepler, to say nothing of Darwin.

On the other hand, turn-of-the-century students at the Harvard Divinity School were confronted with the evolutionary theory as a popular new conceptualization in the intellectual world, and they had to come to terms with Genesis in the light of these assertions.

Similarly today, space probes and space shuttles conjure up still other conceptualizations about the universe into which the traditional stories need to fit. The inbreak of scientific information always creates new contexts for the understanding of the old stories.

But that is a problem that has long been recognized by religious teachers of all faiths down through history. In fact, their major efforts have been concentrated on finding a "now" meaning for the traditional stories—to use current (and overworked) terminology, making the stories "relevant."

Personal Stories as Bearers of Meaning

In all the efforts to contemporize the religious message, to find new meanings for the age-old stories, another set of story-myths has been at work subtly shaping the meaning of faith for each individual. It has been largely overlooked by the religious professionals. This set of story-myths is constructed out of the incidents in the life of the believer forming a unified whole, a life-story, for self-understanding. All of us define ourselves in one way through our experiences. We have a grasp of who we are because we know who we have been.

Our own life history contributes large amounts of content to our life meaning system. Our mothers and fathers, our brothers and sisters, our home life, even our maiden aunts share heavily in helping to create meaning in our lives.

There are, then, two mythologies to contend with. One is the mythology composed of stories filled with meaning from our religious tradition. The second is the set of stories that constitute our own personal mythology. We are constantly logging new experiences in our personal story, dropping some from our consciousness, retaining others for self-understanding.

I do not mean to imply that everybody is influenced by a religious mythology. Nor do I want to convey the idea that religious and personal mythologies are the only significant ones in the building of meaning. We have seen, for example, components in the meaning system built from our identity as Americans.

I do want to show, however, that for the predominant number of people alive today, living in many different cultures, religion is an important contributor to meaning. And most significantly, the stories and images of our personal mythology shape the context in which we receive the religious tradition in which we are reared. We need to attend to the personal story if we want to find out what a person thinks about God. We need to attend to the personal story if we want to see how individuals construe the meaning of their life in this world.

I was started into this area of investigation a number of years ago by a twenty-year-old college student. He stopped into my office one day for a friendly chat, ostensibly about some material we had studied in a theology class. Very soon the mood changed and I found myself involved in a theological discussion about the existence of God.

This was very familiar ground to me. I had heard it many times before. In fact, I think it is one of the few changeless topics in dormitories where all else changes. But there was a difference here. This young man did not believe in God *passionately*. The very idea that there should be a God "in heaven" seemed like a personal insult to him. His feelings were so strong, his language so angry, his emotions so aroused that I knew this was a lot more than the usual testing of the waters, the intellectual inquiry that students sometimes engage in to prepare a new position for themselves. It was not your usual friendly afternoon joust. It was a totally engulfing conflict. I have spoken to many students since then about the same kinds of things, but he topped the scale in the area of feeling.

Since I only knew the young man from class I thought it wise to get a little background, to ask him about his family. I also thought this might soften the focus of the conversation. It did not.

I found out that his mother had died suddenly when he was

twelve years old, leaving him and his two younger brothers. Not long after the mother's death, the father one day dropped them off at their aunt's house for a visit. He never returned.

For a while his aunt tried to care for the three new children in addition to her own. She ended up, however, sending them to a home conducted by Roman Catholic nuns. Tears came to his eyes when he talked about this time in his life. He said he remembered crying in the dining room of the home when he looked over to another table and saw his two younger brothers eating together. He felt sorry for them more than for himself. If his father had not walked out on them they could have been back in their own kitchen having supper. "I never want to see him again," he said about his father. "I hate him." At this point it sounded a lot like his statements about God. I thought there must be a connection. But I was not able to clarify that connection in my own mind at the time.

It was obvious, though, that this period in his personal history was catastrophic for him. His father had abandoned him. So had his aunt, as he saw it. Even his mother had abandoned him in a sense, a feeling that some children have when a parent dies suddenly.

It is not surprising then that any religious teaching about a God who takes care of the ones he loves would not be acceptable in the face of this kind of personal experience. In Christian metaphor God is often referred to as "our Father." The possible association of these two images, God and father, in prayers or religious instructions would also have been very troublesome for him.

It seemed to me at the time that the young man was not questioning the existence of God as much as he was rejecting the kind of God that had been taught to him—the good, caring, loving God. In fact, God seemed to have a greater reality in his mind than in the minds of many of his fellow students who accepted what they heard with a kind of indifferent passivity. His God seemed real, all right, but he must have been more like "the Abandoning One" than the "Caring One" and that was part of his problem.

Threats to Meaning

What happened to this young man was that the meaning system which had been developing normally throughout childhood was suddenly shattered at the age of twelve. The strong bond that once secured him to his mother had been broken. The bond, which he had never questioned, joining him to his father, proved too feeble to hold. His home was dissolved. Suddenly he was alone in the world as he had never been before. The images of God that he learned in connection with the parental bonding tumbled down with the rest.

The breaking of the most significant emotional bond in any person's life is a crisis. It is doubly so when it happens in childhood. It pulls down the main edifice of the meaning system, calling into question all other meanings.

The young man, by engaging me in a long discussion, was beginning the process of rebuilding a meaning system. It would take many discussions and many life experiences before he would be able to position himself again. More importantly, he would not recover a satisfactory meaning system until he could re-establish an emotional bond with someone, rediscover love and rediscover trust. When this happened, I think, he might be prepared to reclaim the caring God of his childhood. This could take years, if it were to happen at all.

Since this incident I have tried to remain alert to the importance of a person's individual life history and its effect on the selective appropriation of religious meanings. In my interviews I have come upon several others who have lost a "significant parent" in childhood. Most of these people do not have a religious meaning system dominated by a *personal* God. It seems almost as if they have been hurt once by the loss of an important *other* and do not want to risk it again.

One of the people who surprised me most was a Roman Catholic nun who had been in the convent for twenty-three years. As a child she suffered the loss of her father. Her mother never remarried. At the age of eighteen she entered the convent and from her first years found herself dodging images of God as Father. It did not appeal to her. Even the image of Christ as a divine person with a "now" reality did not attract her. In her prayer she did not talk to a "One." Her God was a kind of all pervading Presence interpenetrating both people and the physical world. She seemed to swim in a mystical Presence. The divine was very real for her but not personal.

The nun's image of God reminded me of Paul Tillich's views whose works she had never read. Tillich had a problem with the idea of a personal God, and he, too, lost an important parent at the age of seventeen. Tillich's mother was his most significant parent. The psychoanalyst Rollo May, in his brief biography on Tillich, devotes a whole chapter to Tillich's loss of his mother.[7] May, a close friend of Tillich, says that the death was probably the most formative event of Tillich's life.

This fits in with what I have observed in several instances. In Tillich's case I would suggest that the breaking of the deepest emotional bond shocked his meaning system far more than he himself may have realized. Like the others who were unsatisfied with a personal God after undergoing this trauma he set about discovering images of God more in keeping with his experience of life.

Intellectually and professionally Tillich had the tools to articulate a vision of God refashioned out of a damaged meaning system. Emotionally he spent his life searching for a basic bonding with other people, particularly women, and with the physical world itself. He arrived at a kind of nature mysticism that sought the divine in every dimension of earthy reality.[8]

The breaking of the "big bond," whether for the theologian, the nun or the ordinary person, is catastrophic. It either threatens seriously or destroys the life meaning system erected thus far. If an image of God has been built into that meaning system, as it usually is, then it will go down with it. Conversely, when a meaning system needs to be rebuilt, the image of God that accompanies it will have to be congruous with the new system being erected.

In these last examples I have tried to show that each of us brings a personal agenda to the story-myths of faith that are presented to us. Even though the "official socializer," the rabbi, priest or mullah has his own meaning system put together and has a "now" application all worked out for his presentation, the listener may be in an entirely different garden.

Religious educators have usually concentrated on the story-myths of faith, focusing their attention on making them "relevant," that is, giving the traditional stories "now" meanings. I am suggesting that these educators should now inquire into an additional set of story-myths, those that constitute the identity of the listeners. Here they will discover that there are times when no amount of adapting, molding or contemporizing of a story will help. The problems of appropriating religious material lie deep within the person.

Certain story-myths hold dominance within the structure of a meaning system. They have greater significance than others. They gain acceptance because they correlate with the needs, hopes and expectations that have been generated in one's personal history. We are unknowingly selective in choosing the stories that appropriately fit the meaning system that we are making our own.

Summary

In summary, then, I have suggested that meaning systems are all important governors of our lives. They are developed with the aid of story-myths which are the vehicles of meaning. In the religious traditions these stories are changeless, yet they are understood differently by successive generations.

The different understandings are the results of the efforts of theologians and religious teachers to preserve the "now" character of the stories when cultural conditions change. The "now" character is one of three elements that comprise the strong story-myth. A second element is the emotional appeal which helps to bond us to God or to each other. A third element is the pictorial dimension of the story, a vivid visual appeal which helps to imprint the story in our imagination. Which story-myths are appropriated and which gain dominant positions in the meaning system depends upon the unique developments of each person's individual life history.

The individual life story can be enormously influential in the selection and shaping of the images and stories of a religious tradition.

The way we perceive ourselves reflects on the way we receive the stories of our religious heritage. We participate in imaging our God and we participate in imaging the stories that enlighten our life meaning system.

Notes

1. Gordon Allport, *The Individual and His Religion* (N.Y.: The Macmillan Company, 1950) pp. 76ff.

2. Reinhold Niebuhr, *Moral Man and Immoral Society* (N.Y.: Charles Scribner's Sons, 1932) p. 71.

3. Abraham Heschel, *The Prophets,* Vol. I (N.Y.: Harper and Row, 1969), p. v.

4. Viktor Frankl, *Man's Search for Meaning* (Boston: Beacon Press, 1959), p. 117.

5. Myth has many identifications. I make the distinction simple for the sake of clarity. Amos Niven Wilder, *Theopoetic: Theology and the Religious Imagination* (Philadelphia: Fortress, 1976), pp. 73-74, offers eight possible ways of understanding myths.

6. Norman Perrin, *The Resurrection According to Matthew, Mark and Luke* (Philadelphia: Fortress, 1977), pp. 55ff.

7. Rollo May, *Paulus* (N.Y.: Harper & Row, 1973), pp. 37ff.

8. Paul Tillich, *My Search for Absolutes* (N.Y.: Simon & Schuster, 1967), p. 26.

THE POWER OF
IMPRESSIVE EVENTS

Chapter Two

What exactly do I mean when I talk about a life-meaning system? A life-meaning system (hereafter LMS) is an internal orienting of all other participating systems including biological and psychological. It incorporates the values and attitudes that structure reality for each person, giving direction and purpose to human life. It sets a range of priorities from what people consider ultimate to what they think of as trivial. People pursue their daily lives from within the framework of some meaning system.

I use the word system. It is a metaphor. The metaphor connotes both unity and multiplicity engaged in interaction. Within every system, like the circulatory system or even a railroad system, there are inter-relating components, individually discrete, which find their main purpose and usefulness by contributing to the functioning of the whole system.

A red blood cell has its separate unity and identity but it functions appropriately in a total system in which, with others, it achieves larger objectives not possible to it as an isolated unit.

The body itself is a system of systems. It is constituted by the interaction of many participating systems. The psychological system interpenetrates all of the bodily systems with a command center located in the brain.

The LMS informs, guides, governs the totality of systems within the person, giving voice to the most comprehensive expression of the self. It relies upon input from all the systems, correlating them, ordering them and creating a *system of governance.*

A LMS is very difficult to put our finger on, to circumscribe, to pinpoint, yet, like electricity, we know it is there. If it were possible to puzzle out *some* of the main structural elements that contribute to a meaning system and puzzle out their interaction, then counselors and religious educators would have a working model to help them with the people they are called to assist.

Over the past twenty-five years as a religious educator and counselor I have wrestled with the problem of life meaning. In the years since my experience with the college student my search has been more sharply focused. My graduate students and I have interviewed well over a hundred people with the specific objective of getting at the fundamentals of what constitutes a religious LMS. I attempt an analysis of that problem in the light of the knowledge gained from my personal experience and from those interviews.

The brain-center is an instantaneous computer. It retrieves stored information for us at a split second's notice. The use of vocabulary is a startling example of this if we stop to think about it. Thousands of words stand at our disposal ready for use in milliseconds. Our speech flows smoothly as our brain-center effortlessly rummages out specifically apt words to support our conversation. This reveals only our active vocabulary at work. Our passive vocabulary can recognize and understand thousands of more words that are not readily available for active conversation but remain stored for instantaneous recognition.

With the same millisecond accuracy we can recall certain events from our lives that have been significant for us in some way or another and need to be retold again. Ask a person to recall some punishment from his early childhood. Usually within seconds you will hear the sad little details of a story that happened many years ago. Let us take one of those stories and try to analyze it a bit.

The Impressive Event

Raymond is forty-eight years old, a mature, well-balanced high school counselor.[1] I asked him if he could recall ever being punished as a child. "Yes," he said immediately. "It was when I was about nine or ten years old." He then proceeded to tell me the story.

Raymond's father had sent him upstairs to his parents' bedroom to get a handkerchief from a dresser. When Raymond got to the second floor, he met his sister, became engrossed in conversation and forgot completely about his errand. The next thing he knew he felt his father's hand clip the back of his neck a glancing blow. "I thought I sent you for a handkerchief," he chided, got it himself, then left.

Raymond, in describing the incident, gestured with his right hand, pointing out where his father stood in relation to himself and his sister. He added this spatial dimension unthinkingly, mentally recreating the scene.

This is the kind of story parents hate to hear. "My God, what goes into those little computers anyway! Is every thoughtless slap being engraved in stone?" If we were to ask Raymond's father about that incident I doubt if he would remember it. It probably passed out of his "active vocabulary" fifteen minutes after it happened.

But why, given the many corrections that children receive, did this incident surface in a millisecond, retrieved from thirty-eight years before? Was it selected at random? I think not. It required some priority position in Raymond's consciousness for priority retrieval.

Simple as the incident was, I suggest that this was an "impressive event" in Raymond's life. It was not a momentous event, not a traumatic event, not a life-directing event. It was simply "impressive," and by that I mean impressing itself on his consciousness so that it stays in his "active vocabulary." He did not want to forget it.

Impressive events are the ones that people refer to when they talk about themselves. They are occurrences that are remembered easily and seem to be readily at hand for self-description.

If you say to your friends, "What kind of kid were you anyway?" each of them will begin to tell you a story about themselves, conjuring up an impressive event that still tells them who they were as a child.

Of the countless happenings in a person's life only a *relatively* small number are actively retained for one's working vocabulary of self-definition. These we recall in conversations about ourselves whether at a coffee break or responding to the probings of the psychoanalyst.

Let us have a deeper look at Raymond's impressive event. I see in it three factors that are interacting with each other. One is the pictorial character of the incident. Raymond transported himself mentally to his parents' bedroom, knew where the dresser was, knew where he stood in relation to his father and sister. It was a scene on the stage in which he saw himself as one of the characters. He was a central figure, but in a paradoxical way he was also a critic, an onlooker, an assessor. Impressive events all draw on the imagination for a visual reconstruction.

Another element present in the incident is a pattern of emotional bonding that ties together all the players. Raymond was bonded to his father and to his sister. Similarly, both father and sister were bonded to each other. The incident took place in an emotional climate, not intense but sufficient to evoke a slap and cause some embarrassment to Raymond.

The third factor in the piece is the interpretation that Raymond put on the event at the time in which it happened. The slap was a surprise in more than one way. Every impressive event is a surprise of some sort. It discloses something about ourselves that we did not realize before it happened.

In Raymond's case the surprise was the disapproval of his father, whose approval he usually assumed. Additionally, it was the surprise awakened by his own conduct which was normally very much up to expectations, very responsible. How could he mess up such a small errand? That wasn't like him. The triviality of the mission *contributed* to its remembrance. Better store this at the top of the pile for later reference. It goes in the slot that warns against overconfidence in oneself.

The availability of the data for later reference helps explain the third factor that is embedded in the incident. Why is the story still valuable to Raymond? Why not discard it as his father probably did? But the story is still useful. It has a "now" applicability. It helps to explain something about the self right now. It is one tiny vignette, which along with a host of others still says something significant for the self. What does it say? Something like, "I can easily forget my responsibilities. I have to watch myself. I can't let the little things slip." The vignette is small, a tiny image on the canvas of his life, but still necessary as long as Raymond holds on to the view of himself as a responsible adult.

There are three elements present, then, in the incident described: (1) the pictorial character of the scene, (2) the emotional connection in which the subject had important bonds with the others, and (3) the "now" interpretation which continued to give the incident contemporary meaning. These three elements are the basic components of the powerful story-myth that we spoke of in Chapter One.

In Raymond's case the story-myth is, of course, not about God or the meaning of life but simply about himself. He knows a great deal about himself through the many stories that he can tell. Whatever other ways there are of accumulating self-knowledge, this is one of them and one which can be communicated to others rather easily. Autobiographies are filled with stories about the author's experiences. Exploring the impressive events in people's lives is one of the keys to finding out something important about them.

The Landmark Event

There are other kinds of events in people's lives that can help us understand them. I have noticed that some people, in the course of several interviews, repeat the same stories three or four times over. Maybe they just have bad memories!

But then why do they not repeat other stories? Why is it that most stories are told once but a certain select few are told several times over? It seems to me that the person is trying to make sure, in an absent-minded kind of way, that these particular stories be given their full weight.

My method is to give the subjects a long break between sessions, about a month, enough time for them to change frames of reference, to become distanced from the immediate concerns of the last session. In each interview I usually review, in a free-flowing way, a different segment of the person's life. Often enough, the interviewees have forgotten exactly what they have told me in the previous session. They then proceed to tell me some of the same stories over again even though our interview is dealing with a different period in their life.

When this happens we have an event that is filled with more than ordinary meaning. I call stories like this, stories that are repeated several times in the course of a series of interviews, "landmark events." Landmark events often indicate a major enlightenment or a major adjustment in a person's lifestyle.

In the course of four interviews, Sheila, a thirty-five year old

woman, told me three times about an experience she had during adolescence. In one of these interviews she actually underlined it as a
"landmark experience" when she said: "This had more meaning for
me than anything I can think back on."

Well, what was it? First, a bit of background. Sheila had been
baptized a Catholic, the child of a mixed marriage. Her father was
nominally Catholic, while her mother was Protestant. Neither ever
went to church, but on a rare occasion Sheila would go to Mass with
friends. When she did, she did not feel that it was worthwhile. Her
reaction was usually negative. She told me she remembered thinking
on one occasion: "This is all so phony and ritualistic."

Then, at the age of fourteen, Sheila attended a Thanksgiving Day
service with a friend in a small intimate Episcopal church. Her description: "It was so simple compared to what I had experienced before in
a huge church. It was a very nice feeling." I asked her to say a little
more about the feeling. "It was closer; it was a very small group, with
more a feeling of warmth there. For the first time I saw people living
their religion."

That was in one interview. At another time Sheila was trying to
tell me about the way she thought of God. It brought her back again
to that Thanksgiving Day. God seemed to be in the congregation. She
expressed it this way: "It was a people-God feeling instead of a God-
people feeling, if you know what I mean. Something radiated from the
people in this church. I felt the warmth of the church and the power
of God to have people showing this feeling in something." That was a
second interview.

On the third occasion she was telling me about "when going to
church first made some sense to her." Again her explanation is pep-
pered with the word "feeling": "I felt something. I really felt something there." She remembered reaching a kind of conclusion about
church that day, saying to herself: "So this is what it's all about."

Thus there were three statements made at different times, all with
the same tenor of emotion running through them. That day, in a little
church, Sheila had a "landmark experience." Maybe nobody else there
did. She did, simply because it impressed her deeply.

When we hear what is important to other people, it may not
impress us very much. The "landmark events" of others may seem

very ordinary to us. But let us try to analyze it to see whether it marks a high point of clarification for Sheila or a turning point in her young life.

Let us start by reviewing the three factors that participated in Sheila's remembrance. First, there was the visual character of the scene, recreated vividly in her mind. The physical appearance of the church and of the members of the congregation are clear to her. She also recalls exactly where she was sitting during the service.

Secondly, there is the emotional content of the occasion. Surely her repetition of the word "feeling" indicates that strong emotions were involved. It was Thanksgiving Day, always the occasion for warm, grateful feelings.

What about bonding? Does it fit in here anywhere? Curiously, yes. Sheila's parents, the year before, had reunited after a separation of four years. During the separation Sheila lived with her mother. But because her mother was an alcoholic and tried to maintain a job at the same time, Sheila often found herself actually living with other families for long periods of time. Understandably she was lonely and felt rejected on these occasions. It was a very difficult time in her young life.

When her parents got together again she was overjoyed. The whole atmosphere at home changed. Her mother seemed to treat her differently. In fact the emotional bonds joining her to both parents seemed enormously more secure than ever before.

The Thanksgiving Day service crystallized the feelings of acceptance and of bonding in a new setting. The small, closely knit church community welcomed Sheila's participation with genuine acceptance. They were happy to have her as part of the group. These warm greetings broadened the acceptance she had begun to feel at home. Acceptance was experienced in a church community, something she had not known before.

The church group was, in fact, extending an offer to Sheila to become affiliated, that is, to be bound into their community. A short time later she officially became an Episcopalian.

At the time of her experience the feelings of gratitude that normally go with Thanksgiving, joined with the feelings of gratitude that went with the hospitable reception of the group, were sacralized into a prayer. Her prayer flowed directly out of her intense feelings, possibly for the first time in her life. That is why something clicked in her head and she could say, "So this is what it's all about."

What is the third factor in our analysis, the "now" dimension of Sheila's story? Why does she keep the incident alive in her consciousness? For several reasons, I think. First of all, she had found a community to which she could belong, a kind of human and divine acceptance all rolled together. She gained insights into what prayer and church were really about. This formed a high point of awareness for her that she still does not want to forget.

Sheila found her husband in the Episcopal Church, not exactly in this same congregation, because the family moved, but in another similarly warm setting. Among the members of this new congregation she found "a great deal of peace and comfort and feeling and caring."

Sheila has had her share of life's sufferings since then. After ten years of marriage her husband divorced her for another woman. The experience was so traumatic that she wanted to get away from it all. She took her two children and moved out of the parish. She did not need a husband; she did not need a church. She would go it alone. She was thirty years old at the time.

Since then Sheila has pulled herself together but I believe she preserves her "landmark event" as a turning point, in fact, a high point when all systems were go. It signaled a moment when she recognized the acceptance of men and of God. In these terms the incident presents a goal to be achieved again for her, an integration of religion and life that can restore her wholeness and give her a greater measure of peace. The story is of continuing importance to her. She will not forget it.

Here we have a "landmark event" that evidently brings about a major change in direction. It was very subjective, very unique to Sheila. But let us now look at this event from another perspective. Let us look at it from the viewpoint of the congregation.

The congregation had its story, its own particular life history, that made it the way it was. Much as I would like to think otherwise, I cannot imagine every small church group as warm and as accepting as this one. This particular group had built itself this way over the years probably through the efforts of many very kind and caring people. This was its unique way of being a church community, a very attractive one for the newcomer.

Furthermore, this church group was dramatizing a story larger than its own. It was trying to model itself on the "Christian Church" as it ideally perceived that Church to be. In other words, it had a vision of what a good church should be like for the people who belong to it, and it was trying to implement that vision.

The vision was being concretized and offered to Sheila through a bonding process. In effect, the community was saying non-verbally, "Come, share our way of being a Christian community. We want you to be one of us."

This community was an open one. It was willing to share its own particular story as well as its vision of the larger Christian story with this newcomer. In so doing it offered to socialize her into a way of living that had a lot of meaning for her.

The "landmark event" then marked the joining of two stories: (1) the personal story of a teenager in great need of acceptance; (2) the larger story of a social group that knew how to demonstrate acceptance. When the two met, the marriage was consummated, and, I would suggest, a healthy infusion of meaning was given to Sheila's LMS.

Building Blocks of Meaning

Two kinds of stories go into the making of each building block of a LMS. One kind comes from the mythology of the self, a composite drawn from multitudinous experiences. Some of these experiences are of "landmark" significance. They, in themselves, can be sufficiently clarifying to add content to the LMS. Others are more ordinary but still "impressive" events that contribute toward the general shaping of the self-image.

The other kind of story comes from a group larger than the individual, a community that socializes the individual. It has its story, its vision of reality that it treasures as its precious legacy of meaning. It shares this with the ones it loves. This loving and sharing is bonding; it is affiliating; it is the joining of the individual to the community.

I have presented Sheila's story for two reasons. The first was to show the impact of a single "landmark event" on a LMS, given the right set of circumstances. The second was to show that the story of a socializing group need not always be articulated verbally. Certainly, as

Sheila entered into the life of her new community she was to hear many specific verbal presentations of the Christian story-myths. But at the initial level of contact it seems that the acting out of the Christian meaning system was appealing enough in itself to win her affiliation.

There are other examples in which the story-myths of a socializing religious group are presented with great attention to the verbal explanation. In other words, the story itself, in its main lines, touches the listener and clarifies some of the confusions of life for him. The story has such a strong appeal that the listener is willing to accept the invitation to be bound into the group that calls the story its own.

I stress here again that it is not simply an intellectual process. It is also a matter of bonding—bonding to the group that offers affiliation.

There is hardly a more dramatic presentation of the power of a socializing group, with its religious story-myths, than that told by the black leader Malcolm X. Malcolm was captivated by a certain story which he repeated over and over again to win converts for the religion of the Rev. Elijah Muhammad, the black Muslims. It is interesting to note that this is also the story adopted by Cassius Clay when he entered into the black Muslim community and became Muhammad Ali.

The story was told to Malcolm while he was in the Norfolk Prison Colony in Massachusetts by members of his family. He describes its electrifying effect:

> Many a time, I have looked back, trying to assess, just for myself, my first reaction to all this. Every instinct of the ghetto jungle streets, every hustling fox and criminal wolf instinct in me, which would have scoffed at and rejected anything else, was struck numb. It was as though all of that life merely was back there, without any remaining effect or influence.[2]

The story began with the startling awareness for Malcolm that the original man, the first man created by God, was black, not white and that he lived on the African continent.

This black man and his descendants built the earliest civilizations on earth. The white man was a deviant offshoot of this original development. He evolved as the result of a eugenics law devised by a brilliant but evil black man, Mr. Yacub, who set about undermining the creative work of Allah.

Mr. Yacub's law ordered that black babies be put to death at birth but that whenever brownish babies were born they would be reared carefully. As adults they would be permitted to marry each other, thus lightening a whole segment of the population. The matching of lighter and lighter generations finally produced the white man. The resultant white strain of humanity began to cause so much trouble that it was taken to the caves of Europe to fend for itself amid the wild animals. There it furthered its evil ways, surviving by adopting the primitive law of the club and the fang.

The story is a demonology which most religions have. In this case it accounts for the exploitative conduct of whites in their treatment of blacks. Whites were creatures of evil, devils who were never intended to exist in the plan of Allah. This rang a bell in Malcolm's consciousness, so that he began to refer to the "bleached-out" race as white devils.

The story appealed powerfully to Malcolm because it articulated his personal experience of being exploited. His response to the story and to all the aspects of the Muslim faith was total. He immersed himself and his enormous energies in this new commitment.

It is important to look at Malcolm's personal story in order to see how Mr. Yacub's history made sense to him. Malcolm had an image of himself as a person exploited by whites. This image was impressed on him by numerous personal experiences, some of them of "landmark significance."

The earliest, most vivid recollection that Malcolm could recall was a night when he was awakened from sleep by pistol shots when he was only four years old. Amidst fire, shouting and confusion he and his family fled from their burning house, set afire by vigilante white men. He remembers standing in his underwear in the cold night watching his home burn down.

On another night in his childhood he was awakened by the sobbing screams of his mother. He rushed down to the family living room to find it filled with white policemen. His father had been beaten and then thrown under a trolley car. The policemen told him that white men had done it.

Malcolm's mother was left to raise eight children by herself. His life was never the same from then on. His mother's mental health deteriorated. She was then institutionalized. Essentially Malcolm was on his own after that, being looked after by neighbors, then by older brothers and sisters. This was a tragic event of "landmark" significance for Malcolm. It changed the course of his life, forced him to shift for himself and began his life of crime.

A note about Malcolm's father who had been a follower of Marcus Garvey, the organizer of the Universal Negro Improvement Association. This was a back-to-Africa movement for blacks that sprang up in the 1930's. As a preacher, crusader and organizer, Malcolm's father served as an important male role model for Malcolm. He remembers an old lady grinning and saying to his father, "You're scaring these white folks to death." The father represented "negro" rights and found himself often confronting whites.

When Malcolm's father was murdered the LMS that was developing sustained a severe shock. A strong emotional bond had been suddenly severed. Malcolm was only six years old at the time. He then witnessed the rather rapid mental deterioration of his mother. When she was institutionalized a few years later, the bond with her was dramatically weakened. Deprived of these human supports he was, like many others who have lost parents in their childhood, temporarily distrustful of investing further emotional energies in bonding relationships with others.

When the important, bonding components in his LMS were destroyed, the rest went down with them. The meanings that were clearly evidenced in the reality of his parents' lives were taken away. We depend upon the LMS of our parents in childhood. When they are taken away, the living incarnations of meaning, the models of meaning, are removed.

Malcolm recovered meaning through the instrumentality of loved ones, first his brother and sister, then Elijah Muhammad, who wrote to him and sent him money. Yacub's history came with the offer of rebonding, to his family and to the larger community of black Muslims. It helped him recover some of the meaning he had seen modeled in his father. Malcolm became, much more famously than his father, the preacher, the crusader, the organizer whom the white people feared.

The story of Yacub's history appealed to Malcolm not only emotionally but intellectually as well. It is interesting to observe how he checked out the intellectual accuracy of the story. He searched the prison library for Gregor Mendel's *Findings in Genetics* and concluded that Yacub's history could be verified scientifically. You could start with a black man and end up with a white man but not the other way around "because the white chromosome is recessive."[3]

Malcolm also confirmed the geographic origins of the first man as coming from Africa by researching the discoveries of Dr. Louis S.B. Leakey, the British anthropologist.

The story of Yacub's history, therefore, held together for him. He wanted to believe it. He resolved the intellectual questions to his satisfaction, then embraced the black Muslim faith wholeheartedly. The story was no longer "out there"; it had become his own. He had fused with it.

Malcolm's conduct then changed dramatically. He prayed where before he had cursed God. He tried to convert others. His stealing and traffic with women were all over. Even his eating habits changed, for he was now abstaining from pork and giving up smoking and drinking. The new man was symbolized by a new name. Malcolm Little was dead; Malcolm X was born. The transformation could not have been more radical. The "Satan" of the prison, a name given to him by the inmates, had been converted into the saint of Islam.

It is phenomenal that the experience of one momentous event, when everything comes together to make sense out of life, can thereafter be life-governing. But that indicates the importance and the controlling effect of a LMS. In Malcolm's case the story of Yacub's history did not solve all the problems of meaning in his life. It did, however, provide enough of a grasp of the central issues so that it served as a solid working structure, good enough to build upon for the future direction of his life.

With a LMS in place Malcolm was able to exercise higher levels of control over both his biological and psychological systems. He could change his personal habits overnight as anyone can who experiences the intensity of commitment that he did. The new LMS positioned Malcolm in the universe, conferred on him an unsuspected dignity and gave clear purpose to his life. It connected him beautifully with the hero of his early childhood, his father, who was a fearless crusader for the black cause.

A word about Yacub's history. The story-myth has an "other-worldly" character to it which makes it appear outside the everyday experiences of ordinary life. When we ask when this brilliant scientist actually lived we must answer only "sometime in the ancient past." That, in fact, is a special time, a time before reckoning time began. The anthropologist Mircea Eliade, speaking of mythologies, says that these things always happen *ab origine*.[4] Their occurrence becomes normative and thereafter continuously influential in people's lives. Because of the events in Yacub's history back at the beginning, our lives are now the way they are.

Allah in Malcolm's story is much like the Judaeo-Christian God in his otherness. Apart from man, he begins the history of man. But in this case Allah is black, not white. Allah is on the side of the black man in his struggle to regain his proper place in the universe, a struggle that inevitably pits him against whites. While Allah remains elusively other, he nevertheless stands behind the black man as the object of his special concern.

Even though the story-myth has an other-worldly character it speaks of a very real God who has a "now" presence. Even though Allah is elusively other he is nonetheless here and now. That is very important to understanding the religious story-myth in the Western tradition. The "now" presence of Allah makes prayer possible. Once Malcolm perceived the reality of Allah and Allah's plan for the world, he forced himself to his knees in his prison cell and prayed.

It is interesting that Malcolm reflected with some objectivity on the kind of God he worshiped. He was quite conscious that his image of God was different from the God worshiped in the wider black community. He deplored the fact that "the religion of every other people on earth taught its believers of a God with whom they could identify, a God who at least looked like one of their own kind, but the slavemaster injected his Christian religion into this 'Negro.' This 'Negro' was taught to worship an alien God having the same blond hair, pale skin and blue eyes as the slavemaster."[5]

A conviction about the true character of Allah, the black God, and about his "now" presence made total commitment possible for Malcolm. The commitment was a response to the solving of the central meaning of life. When that occurs, as with Malcolm, the commitment is often all-absorbing.

I do not mean to imply that a rational decision is first made and then the emotions are released. It is a unitary process in which both the rational and the emotional participate simultaneously. Commitment comes as an integral part and an essential response to what is perceived as ultimately important in a person's life.

Summary

Let us juxtapose the two lives, those of Malcolm and Sheila, in order to make some concluding observations. Both lives are very different. Yet in their diversity there are certain elements that are common to each of them. These can be helpful in determining how a LMS becomes established and how it achieves life-directing influence. When we analyze the stories we discover: (1) Each person was prepared for the process of religious socialization by the particular events of his or her own life. Within each one's experience a dominance existed which gave a unique contour to the image each had of himself or herself. For Sheila it was her feelings of rejection and isolation which cast a pall over her childhood. For Malcolm it was his feeling of being exploited which began in early childhood and continued through late adolescence. (2) The religious story that was offered to each of them appealed to this specific, dominant self-image. (3) Both permitted themselves to be bonded into a community into which they invested new energies. This involved a changed style of life. (4) The community was able to convey some new meaning about God, a way of discovering what God is "really like." (5) Prayer, which had not been previously part of their lives, entered into their experience as a natural concomitant to their heightened perception of a "now" God. (6) The new life orientations that each assumed added considerable meaning to their lives, giving them a new set of priorities and providing them a greater sense of purpose in their lives.

The LMS is constructed out of the warp of one's personal life experience threaded into the woof of the communal story as one either inherits or comes to know it.

Two sets of stories meld into each other. The personal story is a composite drawn from the landmark and impressive incidents in one's life. The communal story is a composite drawn from the landmark and impressive incidents in the life of the community to which we belong. The special dominance within our personal story seeks out the preferred images and values within the communal story, helping to form the LMS.

Notes

1. All names and information that might identify the subjects have been changed.

2. Malcolm X, *The Autobiography of Malcolm X* (N.Y.: Grove Press, 1964), p. 163.

3. *Autobiography*, p. 175.

4. Mircea Eliade, *The Cosmos and History* (N.Y.: Harper Torchbooks, 1959), p. 21.

5. *Autobiography*, p. 163.

BONDING

Chapter Three

An important part of every "impressive event" and every "landmark event" is the emotional climate in which it occurs. A dramatic moment requires people who have a high degree of feeling for each other or who experience intense emotion on that occasion.

The union that establishes this emotional climate between two people I have referred to as bonding. Bonding links together people who love and care for each other, and it is within the context of bonding that the LMS is built.[1]

Bonding begins as a parent-child relationship and then extends outward to brothers and sisters. As this is occurring the child is being simultaneously bonded into the wider communities to which his or her family belongs. Our interest is in the parent-child bonding and its subsequent effects in bonding into a religious community.

First, parent-child bonding. There are volumes written about the proper parent-child relationship and how this ought to develop under ideal circumstances. It is sufficient for us to note that bonding begins in the womb where the total complexus of systems that constitutes the mother interacts intimately with the total complexus of systems that is the child. These two human centers form a symbiosis of systems that function in resonance with each other.

Bonding is about belonging, and the womb is the symbol of secure belonging. But belonging does not mean being owned; it means being shared. Bonding is about life with a full-time sharer.

Each life sharer creates in the other a solid sense of belonging. Neither experiences the world totally alone. A new mother is a person radically changed in the way she experiences life. She thinks and acts for two. But she is not only a giver; she is a receiver as well. She knows that she has been given a share of another human life that no other person can experience in the same way.

For the child, belonging and sharing establishes a fundamental position of security, a place in this world in which being welcome is a condition of life. Under these circumstances life is transparently meaningful for a child. Fortified with life-sharers like a good mother and father, a baby enjoys the developmental learning tasks that give experiential meaning to life. Grasping, crawling, walking, and speaking are not simply achievements. They are the meaning of life. Delighting parents as well as oneself with these accomplishments makes life exciting and inherently meaningful.

In infancy even though the mother may speak loving words to the child, purely sense impressions are vehicles of meaning. The center of the meaning stage is reserved to smiles, touches, embraces, etc. In the world of the infant these are the impressive events of daily life.

Actually the intensity of these impressions is great. The baby "remembers" but not with the cognitive precision that characterizes the remembering process later on. These experiences are very real ones and very important. Acts of caring are acts of meaning. Meaning resides in the warm bath, tasty mashed carrots and soft blankets given by interactional life-sharers, mom and dad.

There is no doubt that infants who receive such attention actually learn in the process. They learn that they are highly valued. In the language of religion, the Christian religion, this is the first way this child knows about "grace." Being "graced" is the order of the day, every day.

Erik Erikson, the highly respected developmental psychologist, speaks of this ideal human relationship from the infant's point of view as trust.[2] He correctly assesses it as a pre-condition for later religious appreciation.

So it is. But I would like to try to convey more than trust, because I want to connect it with life meaning. I would like to stress the organic continuity of meaning between the mother and the child. The mother knows the history of this relationship literally from its inception. The child's meanings flow out of the biological and psychological rhythms of the mother. Meaning for the infant starts within and continues without, through being tended and touched.

The bond has a unique character for each parent-child pair. The character of the bond is established according to the way in which the caring parent construes the relationship. An example may help. If a baby is born to an exhausted mother who feels abused in her marriage, with this last child just more than she can handle, then this feeling sets the tone of the child's early experience of life. It carries into the feeding, into learning to walk, into all meaning.

Regular food and basic care are not enough for sound bonding. Conscientious nurses who are non-bonders with their "patients" can give food and care. But the nurse does not conceptualize herself as related to an abandoned baby. She does not intend to bond to it, cannot. Hers is not the distillate of a mother's awareness of the deep belonging that exists between parent and child. The nurse's care is conscientious work; the mother's care is working love. Even the exhausted mother is a better bonder than the efficient nurse.

We recall the British children during World War II who were taken from their parents and brought to nurseries in the countryside to be safe from the bombings. Although well cared for physically, many died simply because they were separated from very special sharers who loved them deeply.

Each bond then has its own particular character which is originally shaped by the parent. Each bond also admits of varying degrees of intensity. Not all bonds are equally strong.

The weakly bonded child knows, non-cognitively, that something is wrong in its life yet cannot identify what it is, does not even have the perception to want to identify it.

Weak Bonding Affects Religious Affiliation

The weak bond, like the broken bond, is an obstacle to later religious affiliation. People who give up their family or their faith relatively easily will be found, upon investigation, to have been bonded rather weakly.

One of our interviewees, Marsha, a young woman in her late twenties, can serve as a rather clear example of a weak bond and its repercussions in terms of religious affiliation.

Marsha grew up Jewish, but when she was nineteen she became a Christian. Her objective in doing so was twofold. First, she had met several Christian friends while living away from home and became a convert to be like them, be part of the group. Second, she knew that becoming a Christian would make her parents very angry, and that was just what she wanted. She told her interviewer that it was one way of "getting back at them."

Why get back at them? What had they done? Both were professionals, taken up with their individual careers. Marsha had always felt left out, as if she were an afterthought, a sidelight in their lives. She had little feeling for either father or mother and described them as "wrapped up in themselves."

When Marsha reached eighteen she wrung permission from her parents to live on her own in another city. It was at this time that she met her Christian friends. She has moved among several Christian denominations since then, now attending Roman Catholic Mass, although she does not call herself a Catholic. She believes in Christ but has never felt close to him or close to God in any sense. She is searching for something in Christianity but has not really found it.

In her personal life Marsha has also been searching. She has married twice and has had several lovers. Her second divorce is now in process.

Marsha's searches for the right Christian denomination and the right man are not unrelated. Both are searches for a satisfying bond, a bond that enhances her, makes her feel worthwhile, "graced." She was shortchanged in the bonding process as a child and is paying the price now. Her parents were not able to bond her deeply to themselves or to their religious community, Judaism. Judaism became simply a negotiable commodity to be used against them.

If a child is not bonded deeply and securely to parents we cannot expect a strong affiliation with the parents' communities. By the same token, the tightly bonded child is happy to be part of his or her parents' communities, anxious to become mature members of them.

Strong Bonding Creates Meaning

It is because of bonding that children accept from their parents the interpretations of life that are given on countless occasions. Language, once children have begun to master its mysteries, becomes the privileged vehicle for communicating meaning. Therefore, as soon as children are able to negotiate language, they have two kinds of stories to talk about—their own personal story, the most common in early childhood, and the stories about the communities to which they and their parents belong, more common in later childhood.

In each case the parent serves as the interpreter of meaning. A young mother provided us with an example of this mechanism at work when she was talking about her daughter in nursery school. Note that the child, at the age of four, is interested mainly in her personal story and in her own simple way, with the meanings that are tied up with her personal story.

When little Laurie was picked up at the end of the day she had an incident to report.

"Sarah pushed me. I fell and knocked down Kurt's blocks."

"Why did she push you?" her mother asked. "Did you push her first?"

"No, she wanted my Playdough. She wanted red. I wouldn't give it to her."

"What did you do when she pushed you?"

"I told the teacher."

"That's right. I don't want you ever to be fresh with the other children."

Laurie had an "impressive event" in the nursery school. She retained it until the end of the day. Reporting it to her mother helped her to understand it.

Laurie's mother approved the child's conduct (which she helped to shape in the first place). Her approval re-emphasized her insistence on not hitting other children. Laurie had told her story, had it interpreted in a bonding environment and accepted the lesson.

Values and meaning are learned in incidents like this, insignificant in themselves, piled one on top of the other in children's growing consciousness of themselves.

Meaning is not established the way a house is built, first from foundations, then in an orderly upward fashion to completion. Rather, it is like an impressionist painting on a broad canvas. Strokes and touches here and there pat the landscape, and story after story is layered in, sometimes several in the same area. Sometimes other sections remain untouched for a long while. The dabs build until connections are made and a picture begins to emerge. By the time a person is old enough to critique the painting, using logic and rational principles with a broad overview, the painting is pretty well formed. Revising it in the light of this evaluation is a major growth task in the establishment of meaning.

Laurie's little anecdote had to do with her personal story. My next example shows how the personal story gets fused with the communal religious story very early in the child's life. But in both cases, as I am trying to show, the use of language is essential.

Ricky, who is five, suffered the loss of his grandmother, who was very good to him. In explaining her death he told the interviewer how she went up to heaven.

"She went into a glass box, like a telephone booth. At night she went right up to heaven. She opened the door and got out."

"How did you find that out?"

"My mother told me."

The boy's mother had offered her version of going to heaven modified for five year olds. Obviously, she had not brought Ricky to the burial. The glass box, I suppose, made it less frightening. The mother did manage to convey the idea that the child's grandmother was all right now in heaven and death is not something to fear. I am afraid, though, that she will have to change that story soon. Another year or two and it will no longer be serviceable.

If the mother has to change the story when another relative dies the child will accept it. Bonding carries the day all the time. When children discover that there is no Santa Claus after their parents have backed the story for years, there is no problem if the parents admit it. The "now" situation is so important for children that they are emotionally ready to accept whatever seems correct "now."

Since children's questions are asked within the secure environment of bonding, the answers are received with trust. For the child the answer lies just as much in the parent's attitude, comfortableness, self-confidence, as it does in the words of explanation.

Bonding to the Religious
Community Through Parents

In addition to the personal story, every child is introduced into a community story of some sort, a community wider than the nuclear family. One of these communities is the religious community, and parental bonding is what makes children members. Children are Jews because their parents are Jews, they are Christians because their parents are Christians, they are Moslems because their parents are Moslems. We have to keep that simple fact before us. Parents are the living and concrete connections with these larger religious communities.

From the very beginning a child is an insider in a religious tradition and knows the stories of that tradition as his or her own. It is not the force of logic or of persuasion that makes millions of new Jews, Christians and Moslems. It is the affiliation to their parents. Adult converts from one faith community to another are a miniscule minority in the world's population. Fundamentally, affiliation to a religious tradition remains, for most of the world's population, another expression of love for parents.

Children belong first and learn about their religion as belongers. Christianity's practice of infant baptism is simply a public demonstration of this fact. Belonging is no more a choice than is birth itself. People are summoned into existence by their parents and they are summoned into their parents' communities at birth. Children are also summoned into the constellation of meanings that their parents hold dear. Later, we will deal with how these meanings are individualized.

Children are, of course, not resentful of belonging—surely not before adolescence at least. Their whole inclination is to accept the parents' communal story, their traditions.

The stories, the music, the images are rich embodiments of the heritage which the child is proud of. "What are we, Democrats or Republicans?" second graders will ask their parents at election time. Whatever the answer, that is what they are, and all kinds of good reasons will be found to defend this position with their friends in the schoolyard.

Children often complain about attending CCD classes or going to Hebrew school. Parents wonder whether this is a lack of appreciation for their religious tradition. Maybe the children even complain about attending the religious services themselves.

The sermons and services are long and boring for them, but this has nothing to do with their religious identification or with their emergent meaning system. The services are "understood" in isolation, that is, like the individual dabs of paint in the impressionist painting. In fact, even the religious heritage itself is compartmentalized for the child. "It's great to be a Jew (Catholic) but the services are too long; why don't they cut them in half?"

Religion Does Not Organize
Children's Lives

Keeping the impressionist painting metaphor in mind, picture the pre-adolescent standing right up against the mural, nose to the canvas. He or she sees only a small, immediate area. No overview is possible. The relationship of this small part to the whole cannot be grasped.

Therefore, religion is not the organizer of life for the pre-adolescent, ever. It does not center the lives of children, permeate their meaning system. A mother was horrified when she watched her second grade daughter punch another child on the First Communion line. Afterward, she asked the little girl how she could punch someone and then go in and receive her First Communion. "She stepped on my new shoes," was the answer. In the mind of the child the two incidents were not really related to each other.

It is helpful for us to keep in mind that life, for the pre-adolescent, is a series of vignettes, here and now. Life is by no means tied together rationally any more than it is religiously. The only single factor that systematizes meaning is still bonding, the emotional tie to loved ones. Here is still the focus of meaning until overviews enter the picture with critical thinking and an analysis of relationships.

Importance of Bonding for Parents

Before we leave the topic of bonding there is one more point to be made for it. That is its value in the meaning system of *parents*. Parents find new meanings through being bonded to their children. This bonding even adds impact in the area of religious meaning.

Birth is often a process crammed with meaning for parents. Joyce, a former nun, was overwhelmed by an intense experience of God as she watched her first baby boy being born. Fully conscious during the delivery, she described it as an ecstatic spiritual experience that was not matched by anything she had ever known before in prayer. While the moment was filled with religious "meaning" she could not specify exactly what kind of religious thoughts she had. Her feelings of relatedness to this new child had to do with participating in creation, but that is as close as she could get to articulating how she felt. This moment, however, as a kind of dramatic high point in her life's story when she entered into the creative process, provided her with enormous meaning.

Raising a mentally defective or perhaps deformed child provides almost daily instances in which meaning is challenged in the life of the adult. It is the bonding to the child that intensifies these challenges. It is because it is *my* child who suffers this way that *my* meaning system must respond. The parent is forced to rethink meanings in a way that would never happen if this child were not born.

Much less dramatically, the ceaseless questions of children force parents to retrace their own childhood, this second time around, applying the adult mind to some very basic questions. Children ask the most basic questions when people die, or even when their pets die, or when bad things happen to them. They ask "why" about insects and about school, about sex and about smoking. Because it is *my* child who asks, bonded to me, I try to come up with meanings that are true, good for his or her future, meanings that will set my child straight from the start. It is at this point that parents are confronted with their own meanings, led to decide whether or not they will return to church or let their child live without it, whether or not they really believe in God or will let the child live without hearing about God.

Bonding is an important spur to meaning for adults as for children. Adults who do not have loved ones feel intensely alone and isolated in a way that is not helped by intellectual meanings. One of my graduate students, in taking a life history as part of our research, interviewed a fifty-six-year-old woman who lived in a suburban home alone. Her husband had died a few years before and she had never had children. Margaret was able to support herself nicely and seemed to have no major crises in her life. Each day seemed to be a smooth round of going to work and then returning home to relax. The inquiries that the student made to try to determine what was really crucially important to Margaret proved fruitless. She simply did not feel passionate about anything.

The shocking part of the series of interviews came when the student began investigating Margaret's thoughts about death. Margaret said she would probably die in her late fifties. Surprised, the student asked if she had been sick. No, Margaret said, she was in perfect health. It was just a feeling she had. At fifty-six Margaret had not given herself too much more time to live.

The student came to me quite upset about this segment of the interviews. The data was indeed ominous. The lack of deep interest in anything, the lack of bonding in any depth to any other single person on this earth and Margaret's awareness of it constituted, in my book, a real crisis of meaning.

I received a telephone call from the student about eight months later, after she had completed her degree. Margaret was in the coronary care unit of the local hospital. She had suffered a massive heart attack. Three days later Margaret died. She was fifty-seven years old.

I believe Margaret gave herself a short time to live because she had very little to live for. She was not sharing her life and thus she was not sharing meaning experientially. Her meaning was bound up in her deceased husband, the one person in this world who had meant something to her.

Adults need bonding as well as children. They are helped in their understanding of life by sharers-of-meaning in ways different than children are helped. But adults still need the sharers, the reinforcers of the structures of meaning that they have developed.

In the next chapter I will flesh out some examples of severed or weak bonding. If strong bonding leads children to accept the meanings and values shared by parents, it follows that broken or weak bonds create crisis conditions for the life meanings of children.

Notes

1. I am indebted to Joseph Chilton Pearce, *The Magical Child* (N.Y.: E. P. Dutton, 1977) for my choice of the word "bonding" to characterize the parent-child relationship.

2. Erik Erikson, *Childhood and Society* (N.Y.: W.W. Norton & Company, Inc., 1963), p. 247.

DEFECTIVE BONDING
Chapter Four

The conditions of bonding outlined in the previous chapter are ideal. But bonding is seldom accompanied with that kind of ease. More frequently there are shocks to bonding which jolt and sometimes destroy the relationship entirely. In these instances religious appropriation is either delayed or momentarily stopped.

Death—The Destroyer of Bonding

Death, the death of a deeply loved parent, is the most tragic and the most severe destroyer of the parent-child relationship. It is a crisis in human life that takes bonding completely out of the hands of the helpless, dying parent.

As we have seen in the lives of Malcolm X and Paul Tillich, the death of a parent can be a profound shock to a young person's emerging LMS.

It is important to realize that youthful growth is not simply a matter of physical and mental accomplishments. It is physical and mental accomplishments *appreciated* and *evaluated* by loved ones.

Parents or parent surrogates must interact with the young, growing person. It is their encouragement, response and interpretation that feeds the LMS of the child.

When the parent dies, this important interrelational source of meaning is removed. Every parental death is sudden for a child or adolescent, even after a long illness. It is sudden in the sense that meaning is removed suddenly. The life-sharer who was there yesterday, no matter how sick, is not there today. The parent is permanently gone, never to return.

When this happens, the sense of belonging, once so satisfying and securing, is transformed into a sense of isolation and aloneness. Never again will the child or adolescent have this very necessary life-sharer. *This* source of meaning is gone.

The presence of the other parent, the less favored parent, mitigates the intensity of the feeling of aloneness but it does not eliminate it.

A word about the idea of a "favored parent." Most people say that they are closer to one parent than to the other. It is a way of expressing the stronger emotional bond. Only on rare occasions will an interviewee say that he or she feels equally close to both parents. The bond toward the favored parent is a very special one—one which for the purposes of this study I will endow with a religious term. It is a *sacred* bond. It is the bond that joins two people who revere each other, are in *awe* of each other, need each other. The bond between the favored parent and the child is the precursor of the bond between the child and God in the Western religious tradition.

When the favored parent-child bond is broken by death the emerging LMS of the child is staggered. The relational model which will normally be used to conceptualize and interpret the God-man relationship is also removed. In the face of this blow the immediate task is to recover relationality. This can occur by deepening the bond with the surviving parent or establishing a new bond with another person. The LMS will not be able to build again until the child or adolescent belongs again.

Children and even young adolescents have a difficult time articulating the nature of the loss. They know that the death of their father or mother has left them deeply empty and alone but they are not usually aware of the blow to life meaning.

The damage will become more evident during the task of personal appropriation. This will provide a number of difficulties for religious faith because the original task of normal appropriation was interrupted, disoriented.

Religious educators and counselors who deal with adolescents will act wisely if they inquire into the home situation of youngsters who have extraordinary difficulties with their faith. Sometimes counselors will spend their time trying to clarify points of faith, precisioning theological ideas, when the problem lies in a much deeper, emotional area, the area of bonding which may have been damaged several years before.

Divorce Similar to Death

Bonding is also seriously damaged by divorce. Next to the loss in death, divorce is the most punishing physical separation that a child can experience. Because of the extensive divorce rate this is now the number one cause of bonding problems.

In divorce the absence of the unique life-sharer again leaves the child devastatingly alone. The fundamental attitude of belonging is disrupted. All the meaning that resided with the approving and enlightening presence of the favored parent is suddenly threatened. Visiting rights are a poor substitute for the ongoing presence of the favored parent. The interpretation of life's events cannot be relegated to a Sunday afternoon.

The situation is worsened when the favored parent remarries and, it seems to the child, permanently "belongs" in another family. The other parent subsequently remarries and forms still another family configuration.

This new "extended family," the creation of divorce and remarriage, generates a unique meaning problem for children. Each parent belongs with a new partner but the child feels short-changed in the transactions. He or she seems to belong less to either of the two parents.

Two things happen. First, the child suffers the consequences of loss, similar to that experienced at death, regret, guilt, anger, or depression. There are complaints to both parents about the new situation. Second, there is the desire and the need to belong again. But with it there is fear and hesitancy lest attempts at new relationships suffer the same fate as the sacred bond. The capacity for commitment is endangered, at least temporarily.

A commitment to people, though eagerly desired, will not be readily accomplished. Similarly the commitment to God which is called for by the Western religious traditions, a commitment which is understood fundamentally in relational terms, will not be appreciated. To put the whole thing in very stark terms, the child who has lost a

Bonding Relationships
Mother as Favored Parent
Before Divorce

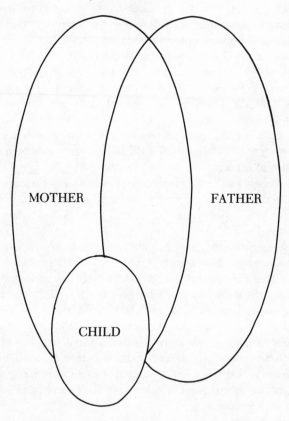

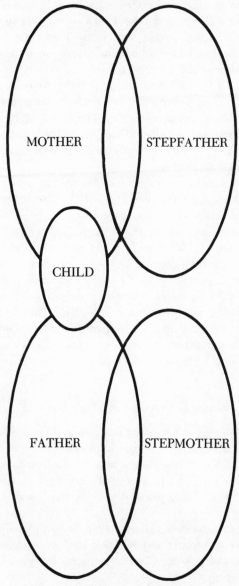

Mother as Favored Parent
After Divorce and Remarriage

MOTHER

STEPFATHER

CHILD

FATHER

STEPMOTHER

Each Parent "Belongs" to a New Partner

favored parent by death or divorce has lost his or her share in a "sacred union." Before a new sacred union with God can be effected successfully a second "sacred" union with humankind must heal the first wound. The bond with God is built analogously upon the experienced bond with humankind.

In awarding the custody of children in divorce cases judges often overlook the favored parent status when it involves a child and his or her father. This can be truly damaging. The father can be just as easily the favored parent as the mother. There should not be a routine awarding of the child to the mother simply because children are supposed to be reared with their mothers.

I have stressed the importance of the favored parent. Divorce is *not* so devastating when the child goes with the favored parent. But it may become so when this favored parent remarries and that new relationship *seems* to the child to threaten the "sacred" bond. It is the mere threat to meaning that is not healthy and needs to be resolved early.

Any major disruption in the life of parents, like a mental breakdown or alcoholism, will inhibit the establishment of secure bonding. The alcoholic parent is erratic, cannot be counted on, often provides a living model of meaninglessness to the child. Thus consistent and authentic life-sharing between this parent and the child becomes impossible. We can expect under these circumstances that the establishment of a solid LMS will be delayed because of these difficulties.

Sexual Differences in Weak Bonding

Girls who have been inadequately bonded often seek out early marriages. Their objective is to abandon a home situation that is emotionally unsatisfying. Envisioning a new bonding relationship with a husband who will supply the emotional security they lack, they are unaware that they bring their disability with them to the new relationship.

Wanting to commit themselves wholly to another person they are somehow prevented from doing so. These kinds of marriages and relationships cannot often survive the adjustments necessary in the early years and break up.

Bonding to another is a difficult lesson to learn when not first experienced in childhood. It may take several other relationships to puzzle it out if it is unraveled at all.

Boys who have been inadequately bonded do not react in exactly the same way. Rather than commiting themselves to individuals about whom they are supercautious, they are more likely to commit themselves to institutions or organizations that offer the prospect of secure belonging. They join the navy, or gangs, or even enter a seminary in their late teens.

Interestingly, I have interviewed seven people who have become priests or nuns and who have had an alcoholic parent. I do not want to generalize from this small segment, but in each case they definitely seemed to want to get away from home. They seemed to be looking for a more meaningful life and for bonding, the prospects for both seeming great in the service of God.

This form of life, with its ideals, its order and daily regimen, was in dramatic contrast to their homes where there was often the chaos of meaninglessness during a parent's alcoholic sessions.

The search for both meaning and bonding in this context is as difficult as it is for the adolescent prematurely married. The root of the problem lies within the self, and that fact is not often discovered until sufficient life experience is logged, perhaps into the early thirties.

Weak bonding, for whatever reasons, is a hindrance to deep religious affiliation and religious experience. Being "graced" is a basic human experience that has been inadequately experienced in these lives. Therefore, the young person, attempting to intellectually conjure up what it means to be loved by God, is trying to identify a phenomenon that remains, in large part, outside the ambit of his or her experience.

The Unbonded: Religious Affiliations Are Difficult

There is a very small percentage of people who seem never to have been bonded to parents at all. Because of unique circumstances, unwanted in a single parent household, raised in foster homes, abandoned and raised by a variety of caretakers, these children grow up feeling that they belong to no one. Since bonding supplies meaning in infancy and childhood, these children are without a solid grasp on meaning. A LMS will be very slow in being puzzled out, if a coherent unity is ever reached in their lives at all. Religious commitment, if it comes, will follow the gift of "grace" which is a bonding situation established with someone who is fully versed in bonding in his or her own life.

Home Is the Bonding Environment[1]

Huston Smith has an essay on the effect that nature has upon the religious perception of peoples. He cites the unpredictability of the Yellow and Yangtze Rivers in China with the Chinese unwillingness to believe that nature can be ultimately controlled. In contrast, he offers the Middle East's "Fertile Crescent," an area watered by the Tigris and Euphrates Rivers, as more manageable and an area more representative of God's beneficence.

Smith's point is that the natural environment is an important factor influencing the character and style of religious belief. Analogously, the home is a centrally influential environment for the interpretation of human and religious experience.

The home is where the first bonding takes place and where the child is first introduced to God. In Judaism, Christianity and Islam that *God is one* and is a specific person. He is separate and distinct. But so is the child. The three religions teach that the distinctiveness of both God and humankind is never compromised no matter how intimate their union. A human being never fuses into God even in heaven.

The task, then, of being bonded to God is just like the psychological task that challenges each individual, to be joined and bonded yet remain autonomous, to be free but to also freely commit oneself to another.

The meaning of religion in the Western traditions is belonging to God, being related. But how can one know what a relationship to God is like if the relationship with the most important human being on earth (one's parent) is thrown into doubt or confusion or, worse still, is non-existent? The child is too absorbed in trying to find a reliable life-sharer to take on the more remote possibility of discovering a relationship to God.

The very first and essential task in religious education, bonding, does not seem "religious." But it is the foundation for religious experience and for the formation of a secure LMS. God is introduced, incarnated and kept alive through the convincing power of parental love in the bonding process. In this beneficent environment the first symbolic acceptance occurs. It remains for children to appropriate as life goes on, to come into their own freedom and make the individual commitment that affirms the tradition that they at first uncritically received. Bonding to parents is preserved. Bonding to God is preserved and positively reaffirmed.

The ideal conditions are clear. Equally clear are the problems that result from defective bonding or no bonding at all. But what about families where parents dearly love their children, where the children know secure belonging, are bonded successfully, but are not closely affiliated to a religious tradition?

Julie, a twenty-six-year-old graduate of a Catholic college, might be a good example of this kind of person. Julie's parents tried to do everything right for her. Well educated themselves, they were very conscious of their responsibilities as parents, giving Julie love, attention and a careful upbringing. Religiously they were Roman Catholics, rather minimal in their observance. They attended Mass on Christmas and Easter and occasionally on Sundays, but the details of holy days, fasts, home prayers and individual religious practices were disregarded. They had many "gripes" against the Church but chalked them up to the human dimension in the institution. They could not get too excited one way or the other.

While Catholicism was their story they were not deeply and emotionally invested in it. Julie was enrolled in a Catholic college with a good academic reputation not for faith reasons but because they thought it provided a more disciplined and moral environment.

Julie had other reasons for going. Among them was the desire to feel part of the Catholic community and to learn something about her religion that would help her personally.

It did not happen. The religious attitudes she brought from home, which she did not express openly, made her feel like an outsider when she compared herself to the other students. The religion courses were few and did not stimulate her to any further commitment.

After graduation Julie married a young man whom she had met in college. His religious background was not unlike hers. A former Catholic, he had "found Christ" in a small evangelical sect and had become deeply involved with the group. His enthusiasm washed onto Julie. Soon she was attending services and eventually joined the community.

Julie's decision toward this religious commitment gave a strong new direction to her life. Her sense of purpose and meaning were strengthened through her marriage and through her new attachment to this church. She felt she had now learned to pray. She brings her infant son to the services and, it seems clear, will bond him into an amended version of the communal story she grew up with throughout her childhood.

Three observations seem pertinent with regard to Julie's case. First, bonding within her family of origin had been strong. Therefore, the major pre-condition for bonding to God—in this instance, through active acceptance of religious faith—had been met. Yet, because her parents were not deeply and emotionally committed Catholics themselves, they could not share a deep conviction with her. Her decision had to wait for a caring community to invite and encourage her to belong. This happened through the instrumentality of her husband.

Second, reappropriation was not a major task for her because the original religious appropriation was not strong to begin with. College did not generate the stimulating environment for reappropriation according to Julie's specific needs, so she did not invest much psychic energy into it.

Third, Julie changed her faith stance not because of cogent intellectual strengths in her new story or because of intolerable weaknesses in the old but because bonding to her husband created the positive environment for the acceptance of his new-found faith. She probably would not have taken on her new beliefs if her girlfriend, instead of her husband, had found Christ in this sect.

Bonding by Parents
Without Religious Affiliation

A bonding situation similar to Julie's exists when parents show their children deep affection and care but have *no* religious affiliation at all. These are the parents who bond their children securely giving them all the love they need but have no identification with a religious tradition to offer them as the basis for a meaning system. Children "belong" but their belongingness is limited to the immediacy of their own families. These are the young people, who in their twenties are looking for a community and a cause wider than the family.

The thrust of the basic human need is for belonging. People want to belong and they want their belonging to have significance and meaning. Therefore, once the parental bond is properly established, the desire is to broaden one's affiliation toward other individuals and toward a community that can share life meaning and direction. The search is for a community that can give articulation to the kind of meaning one has already experienced through bonding while growing up.

These are the kinds of young people who commit themselves to religious groups with a strong community sense. Many of them are very bright, yet they, in the beginning at least, do not require an elaborate theology. They need, first and foremost, a caring group with a strong ideal, a direction and a sense of purpose. This makes them part of a community which has a grasp on life meaning. Life-sharers are in abundance reinforcing each other. That is important for the searching young adult, especially when life-sharing has previously lacked the religious dimension. It is almost as if time has to be made up, as if a void must be filled in order to be whole.

I am suggesting, then, that when the essential task of parental bonding has been done well, even if there has been no religious education accompanying it, the person so bonded is an ideal subject for religious affiliation. Religious educators and counselors find these people a delight to work with because of their genuine interest and motivation.

Bonding by Parents of Different Faiths

One last situation exists regarding bonding that is worthy of note. It is the situation in which both parents lavish love and care and bond the child properly but are of different religious persuasions.

Michele, whose father was a Catholic and whose mother was a Jew, was told from as far back as she could remember that her religious choice would be left entirely to her. But in practical terms this meant that while she was growing up she did not belong to either the Catholic Church or the Jewish community. She had decisively neither the communal story nor the traditions of Judaism or of Christianity. For example, she was in the anomalous situation of receiving presents and having a Christmas tree but not accepting the Christmas story as her own. She would go to a relative's house for Passover but not have the meal in her own. Other kids knew exactly what they were. She did not, and it bothered her very much.

Michele also knew without either parent ever saying so that each one wanted her to decide in their favor. She was in the middle of an unmentioned conflict, a silent tug-of-war.

Her parents were unable to tell their individual stories by common agreement. Therefore, they were unable to be life sharers in an important area of life. For Michele this was unreal because both of her parents were reluctant to share what was an important part of them and the foundation of their LMS.

When Michele reached her teen years her dissatisfaction was heightened by a series of other home problems. Her relationship with her father became severely strained. To relieve the tensions she went to live with her mother's relatives for a while.

This was the turning point. They were Jewish and offered her understanding and acceptance. Michele, with relief and joy, embraced her Jewish identity. She convinced herself by the logic that the child of a Jewish mother is supposed to be Jewish. The new commitment settled and positioned her—at least for a few years. At least this was religious appropriation. The difficult task of integration would come later.

In a mixed marriage the religious decision should be made for a child at birth. Then in their own minds each parent is clear about what will happen in the process of religious acculturation. The parent whose faith the child will share can feel secure that he or she can communicate his or her own stance with confidence. The child will have an identity and a sense of belonging in every way right from the beginning.

This does not avoid problems, of course. There is always the possibility that the favored parent will turn out to be the one of the other faith. We do not know favored parents at birth. But if that is the case, at least the lines of difference are clearly drawn. When the child is old enough this parent can explain his or her position and the reasons for maintaining it. Positions will be clearly in the open and at the very least communication about religious traditions and beliefs can be aired in the loving environment.

Summary

To summarize what I have intended to say in this chapter, the LMS of the child is, at first, a borrowed one. The meanings reside with the parents and, if they are believers, are bound up in the stories that dramatize and explain their religious heritage.

The child accepts the heritage because he or she is bound to the parents by the totalizing ties of intercommunication and love. Very early in life the child begins to develop his or her own personal story. During this development, meaning is still borrowed from parents who by their encouragement of growth accomplishments, their care and their support communicate a sense of purpose to the child.

Language as it develops becomes the instrument for the interpretation of meaning and value. The child can begin to tell his or her personal story and the parents can react to it in ways that are clearly understood.

God becomes real through the mediation of parents. In childhood God is one among many meanings, not the giver of all meaning. Parents help to determine the importance of the divine.

As the skills of relating to others are refined, children are introduced into the broader community to which they know they already belong. This is their church or synagogue. These are people with whom they belong. The stories from home are heard in a wider context of people, uncritically accepted. What has been heard at home has also been heard outside. It seems that everybody has the same story.

But the first days in school change that. Children identify themselves by other designations. Some are Catholics, some are Jews, some are Methodists. But the children hold firmly and solidly to what they are and find all kinds of good reasons for being that.

Appropriation begins in early adolescence, as an "insider" but with a more critical look at the tradition. Positive acceptance and affirmation is the inclination, though reason and good sense demand a hearing. Sometimes rejection is necessary but without upsetting the bonding that joins the youngster to parents.

Bonding is the bearer of meaning through childhood and into adolescence. It continues to tie young people into their tradition emotionally even as the calculus of reason finds difficulties with some of the stories. The power of the tradition binds through the strength of loving parents who supply the main source of meaning even into the young adult years.

Note

1. Huston Smith, "Accents of the World's Religions," in John Bowman (ed.), *Comparative Religion* (Leiden: Brill, 1972).

THE GOD-IMAGE IN THE RELIGIOUS STORY

Chapter Five

It is clear that bonding not only binds children to the parents, but it binds children into the parents' communal stories. Accepting the parental communal stories, children build their LMS by melding their own personal story with these communal stories.

Therefore, the LMS is shaped, regarding what is of ultimate and unrestricted value through the interaction of the personal story with the communal story. It is at this point that we meet the question of God in the LMS of those who espouse the Western religious traditions.

According to the communal story of Jews, Christians and Moslems ultimacy resides with God. That is, God is the most important reality whose plan in creation is carried out as the central activity in the universe. God began all things and conducts the happenings in the universe in keeping with his own purposes. Our task is to acknowledge this ultimacy, respond to the divine initiatives in our lives and thus fulfill our purpose in the divine plan.

But in each of the three religious traditions people are not insignificant. They have high status and value before God. In fact, they are a "little less than a god" (Psalm 8) in their stewardship and control over lesser creatures.

Christianity further elevates the status of humankind, seeing in Jesus the perfect harmonious interaction of the divine with the human. Jesus becomes the model for human possibilities, the symbol of the bonding of people to God.

Notice that ultimacy in Judaism, Christianity and Islam resides with God who is outside of the self. No matter how close the union, God and humankind remain distinguished. Ultimacy resides with God, with Christ or with Allah. The divine reality stands as the central and most important of all realities, whether or not that fact is acknowledged by other peoples.

The Personal Mythology

But there is another story that urges ultimacy upon us. It is our personal story made up of the unique incidents and activities of our lives. These incidents are the individual story-myths linked together in our awareness of ourselves. Their accumulation constitutes the personal mythology which is uniquely ours.

Our parents usually begin this mythology for us. They tell us the story of our birth. It may go something like this: "You were premature. so tiny you had to spend extra time in the hospital. We even worried that you might die. When we finally got you home we stayed up many nights with you to give you your regular feedings, etc."

A characterization like this is true mythology. It has the visual content of a story, it has the emotional associations, the bondings, and it has a "now" dimension. The "now" dimension means to the parents and to the child that they took extra special care of this little one. The baby was tiny and weak, but because of the parents' loving care it is now big and strong. The parents stand ready to continue to give the extra attention and care necessary because this child is special.

Almost everybody has a birth story about themselves. Either they came as a special blessing from God to parents who could not have a baby or they were so good that they never cried (or the opposite and they are still a pest).

Parents have favorite stories about our early childhood, about our adolescence and our adult years. We take over our own mythology as soon as we are able to. We remember what we want to about ourselves, the stories that help to remind us who we are and what we are like.

Whatever the special circumstances of our lives, no matter how poor or deprived. looking out from our own centers, it seems that, of all the people on this earth, we are the most important.

This kind of mythology assumes that the really significant occurrence in world history took place when *we* entered this world. Before that, there may have been big doings but they are strangely distant and not very important for us. Similarly, we do not like to imagine the world going on for any great length of time once we are dead. That would seem anticlimactic.

When we put this vision of reality into religious terms we can say that we are of ultimate significance for ourselves. At least that is the practical result of the accumulation of stories about ourselves and the ongoing experience of living.

In this case the appeal for ultimacy does not lie outside of ourselves with an "external" God but within ourselves. The net result is that two sets of stories call for ultimacy, one from the religious group that socialized us and the other from the sheer experience of living.

The Blending of the
Personal and Religious Stories

Once the ultimacies are relatively positioned (and I see this as an ongoing life process) the LMS calls all the other systems into cooperation in living out the priority structure. The LMS, when settled into its grasp of what is ultimate, makes day to day life decisions based on the grasp of reality that it has accepted.

Let us take a look at the martyrs of the early Christian Church, and their modern counterparts, to see how the two bids for ultimate value can function together in a single system.

The martyrs, then and now, know that the ultimate reality is God. He sees their every action and calls them to fidelity. If death is what is required under certain circumstances and there is no other option short of infidelity to conscience, then death is the choice. God is present and supportive in the decision.

In permitting their lives to be taken, however, the martyrs do not expect to be snuffed out of existence. They expect that the God who sees them in their final hour will be the God who takes them to himself moments later.

In this moment of heroic self-giving, of letting go of the world, the martyrs do not let go of themselves, of their ultimate survival. "Life is changed, not taken away."

They continue their historic existence. Something of the ultimacy of the self is preserved. The two ultimacies are harmonized.

Put the same issue into an entirely different religious tradition. Look at the interplay of the personal story with the communal story in the Hindu idea of reincarnation. Pious Hindus can accept death with tranquility, and they often welcome it if the circumstances of life are wretched enough. Death does not threaten the ultimacy of the self. It is not a total dissolution in which one vaporizes into nothingness. The Hindu faith-myth assures them that another lifetime awaits them with all the possibilities of a better existence. At the same time their personal mythology is satisfied that it will continue on by simply passing through the mysterious transition that is death.

Most people on this earth are presented with two sets of ultimacies in the process of growing up. Both are of unrestricted value. One is taught to us by our socializing group. The other we learn through the experience of living. Parents are usually deeply involved in the generating of both and are not explicit about their potential conflict.

The LMS correlates the two sets of stories arriving at a unique system that makes sense, fusing together information from both sources. A system of governance is developed which serves as a guide to prioritizing values. It determines what is central, what is of major importance and what takes precedence in the ordinary occurrences of life.

Official religious story myths in Judaism, Christianity and Islam position God and man within dramas which serve as models for establishing ultimacy. The dramas are the stories we have all heard in the reading of our Scriptures. In these dramas God is usually imaged according to the central thrust of the religious tradition. For example, in Judaism and Islam the transcendence of God is normally stressed, while in Christianity his immanence is in the forefront. Other models of God are, of course, presented that do not fit these categories. They try to capture the many facets of the divine as each tradition preserves them.

Blending the God-Image from the
Personal and Communal Stories

Keeping in mind that there are many official images of God presented by the Scriptures of each tradition, let us turn the main focus of our attention to the *subjective* appropriation of these images as they affect the individual. After all, it is the specific and favored God-image that *I* appropriate that becomes the cornerstone of *my* understanding of God no matter what other images there are out there in the tradition. My God-image is tailor-made as I selectively appropriate it, and it is this image that serves in the setting of priorities for the LMS. That is the subject of this chapter. In the following chapter I will study humankind's part as presented in the religious dramas and show how this correlates with the divine imagery we individually accept for ourselves out of the many images available in each religious tradition.

Each tradition has its own parameters. For example, the story myths of Judaism provide many images of God, yet they do not provide an image of the divine in the form of a man who walks the face of the earth as a flesh and blood human being. Christianity offers that exact image in the person of Jesus Christ. Islam does not offer it and specifically rejects it in the Koran.[1] A Jew does not have the Jesus-image to choose from, nor does a Moslem. Christianity has a plethora of images to choose from; some, like the images associated with the Holy Spirit, even provide for the possibility of a non-personal view of God.

It is the task of the deepest core of the self to appropriate an image of God that is consistent with the many proffered images offered by the religious tradition to which he or she is affiliated, selecting this image in keeping with the dominances of one's personal story.

A brief preliminary word about "God-images." I prefer that term to the more popularly used "God model."[2] The word "image" has associations with the psychological community rather than with the community of natural scientists, and this seems more appropriate to a discussion of the mysteries of the interior of man.

Furthermore, an image can be connected with an internal impression, and that is more congruous with the schema that I am presenting. A number of impressions help to create an image. So with all due respect to several distinguished scholars who refer to "God models," let us work with the word "image" and try to establish the position of the God-image within a LMS.

I propose two cases for study as examples of the establishment of a favored God-image. In the first instance, the God-image of the subject, David, was firmly established within the parental matrix. In the second, with Ellen, the God-image was formed in the setting of parent surrogates.

David's God-Image

David's upbringing represents a classic example of strong bonding accompanied by the formation of a God-image in a deeply religious home. David is now in his late thirties and readily speaks of the warm love and affection that he received from both of his parents. In our interview he repeated without hesitation his father's typical blessing. His father was a rabbi and a model of what faith was supposed to be. The blessing went this way: "May you live to be a pious individual, become saintly and scholarly and fulfill the ways of our ancestors."

David remembers going with his father to the community center for exercises and a steam bath, and then directly to the synagogue for services. The two worlds, physical and spiritual, flowed together, as he put it.

David's father always found time to spend with him no matter how busy he was. He recalls instances of his father's attention and concern. But all of life was interpreted in religious terms. There were no "secular" reasons for things happening in the world. God was in charge of all, and, as David remembers, "everything in life was viewed from a religious point of view."

It was in this caring environment thoroughly penetrated with a faith point of view that David, the only son in the family, grew up. At a later moment in the interview I came around to discussing the way in which he looked upon God. This was David's description of God: "God is a superfather kind of image who really does give a hang and has the time and patience to be concerned with me as a human being. I always feel I can approach him with confidence."

Later, and in another context he said of God: "I know I will be treated as any father treats a child—with love."

David's God-image is, of course, remarkably like his own father. The image of God as Father is also found within the Jewish Scriptures as one image among many. It would not be characterized as the most prevailing or pronounced image. But it was there for David to choose from, and his father fleshed out that imagery in real life. So David easily chose "father" as a favored image of God.

David, like his father, is also a rabbi, living out, almost literally, the words of his father's blessing. He says he tries to instill the same devotion and fidelity to faith in his own children as he received it in his home. As this example shows, faith lives from generation to generation through the strong influence of parental faith-sharers.

People familiar with the writings of Sigmund Freud may say that David's case falls clearly under the categories outlined in such books as *Totem and Taboo* (Vienna, 1913) and *The Future of an Illusion* (N.Y.: Doubleday, 1961). In these works Freud presents the religious person at a childish stage of development creating an image of a god as a father who will help him cope with the threats to existence just as a father helps his child. The religious person creates God out of the longing for strength and support that he finds lacking in this world. The father metaphor fits this need best.

Therefore, David accepts the image of God as Father because he is grown up now; he cannot rely upon his father in the same way that he did as a child, so he is content to project a father in another dimension and look beyond the earth for understanding and strength.

Not to become overly concerned here with Freud's thesis, I offer two brief observations. First of all, I agree with one part of the Freudian speculation. I think we do project an image of God in our minds, appropriating the God-image that best correlates with the experiences of our lives. The image of God we accept, although selected from a "pool" of possibilities offered by our religious tradition, has a uniqueness to each of us which we have had a share in making.

Secondly, I think Freud basically misreads the character of the religious person. The religious person at the core usually is not the threatened human being, the one who lives in a hostile world, desperately in need of help. Freud may have encountered a disproportionate share of people like this because of the nature of his practice. The religious person, like David, for example, is a belonger. He or she belongs with caring parents, feels welcome in this world, fits almost organically into life. This kind of person is not a stranger in an alien land but a participant with a rightful and established role in the world.

God, then, is not simply the supplier of desired needs, although he is also that. God is the other side of the human equation, the other important one (next to the self) in the story-myth of life. The divine is a focal point of meaning for the religious person. God is integral to a LMS for the religious person.

Enough for Freud for the moment. Back to David. His view of God as Father is preferred to all others. It is preferred not only because that image correlates with an important parent but because the family metaphor best explains what is happening between God and people and between individual people in this world.

The family, which he knows from his personal experience, is a microcosm of total life. Thus David fits into it, and, analogously, so does God as Father. The human race is one family, often disjointed but ideally directed toward reaching some form of love and unity.

The God-image, in David's case as Father, while internal and unitary, can be thought of as having two characteristics. These I propose to call simply "non-cognitive" and "cognitive."

The non-cognitive character has to do with feelings, with emotions. It is how we feel toward God as a result of the association of a particular image. For example, David's feeling toward God is similar to his feeling for his father because it has been transferred from his relationship to his father.

The "feeling" aspect of religious experience, though very common, is not easy to describe in precise words. Rudolph Otto in his classic study *The Idea of the Holy* (Harper, 1958) spoke of the non-rational elements of the sacred.[3] These are feelings that defy exact description. Otto spoke of the feeling of creatureliness, of awefulness, of being overpowered, of being aware of mystery.

How does one describe awe? How do we articulate a degree of intensity within the feeling of creatureliness? How do we say exactly how we feel when overwhelmed by the divine presence?

Feelings have many dimensions. My point is that these feelings, in David's case, about the fatherhood of God have unique emotional dimensions specific to David and to his relationship to his father. These are tailor-made for him, just as the God-image itself was tailor-made. Not every image of God as Father has the same emotional connotations.

What about the cognitive content of the father image? Cognitively, everybody knows what a father is. It is a man who is parent to the child. Within the broad parameters of that definition many variations are possible. The cognitive image is like the musical key that sets the tone for the limitless possibilities within that key. There can be many variations within the fatherhood image but fatherhood sets the pattern.

In religious literature images of God abound. Our first meeting with these images is in their cognitive dimension. Let me illustrate this by taking a segment from Psalm 68:4-5. The reader of the psalm is invited to praise God under a variety of images:

> . . . extol him who rides over the desert plains.
> Be joyful and exult before him,
> father of the fatherless, the widow's champion,
> God in his holy dwelling place.
> God gives the friendless a home
> and brings out the prisoner safe and sound.
>
> *(New English Bible)*

Six different images of God tumble from the psalmist's lips and are captured succinctly in a few sentences. They are set before us by the skillful selection of highly descriptive words. We meet them cognitively, intellectually, at first. God is a desert rider. a father to the orphan, a friend to the widow, a powerful one in his palace, a benefactor to the homeless and a freer of captives.

The emotional associations will then be made by the readers when they are able *to identify* with one or other of the images. Are the readers orphans? Then they will feel an affinity to the image of God as "Father of the fatherless." The emotional associations represent the non-cognitive dimension of the God-image. The cognitive dimension is set by the descriptive metaphor.

Ellen's God-Image

Earlier I said we would take two cases in our study of the development of a God-image. Let us now move to the second and in so doing further clarify the distinction between cognitive and non-cognitive in the God-image.

Ellen is thirty years old, the mother of four children, and the sister of Sheila, whom I mentioned in an earlier example. Ellen was three when her parents separated. From that time and until she was eight she stayed with several sets of foster parents.

The last surrogate parents that Ellen lived with were a Presbyterian minister and his wife, both of whom Ellen loved very much. They, of course, took her to church and Bible school every Sunday. She felt very loved at this time in her life and spoke enthusiastically about her "fantastic Bible school in the summer time." They were forever playing games and singing hymns. She enjoyed both immensely.

Ellen learned only many years later, as an adult, that the minister and his wife had lost their only daughter just before Ellen came to live with them. Obviously they had transferred much of their love to her. They needed her as much as she needed them. The emotional bond became so strong that Ellen remembers how sad she felt, how filled with tears and sorrow when she went to rejoin her own parents who were getting back together again. She was eight years old and she still remembers thinking that it did not matter to her that her parents were reuniting. She loved the minister and his wife.

The minister had given her a Bible which she treasured. In it there were many pictures, but one in particular fascinated her. She spoke of it several times in her interviews. It was a picture of Jesus holding a cute little lamb in his arms. He was the Good Shepherd.

When Ellen returned to her parents she still thought of herself as belonging to the same church as her surrogate parents though she did not attend it. Her family lived at a distance, and neither her mother nor her father went to any church. When Ellen was old enough to go to church by herself she sought out a Presbyterian church but was deeply disappointed. She felt no warmth there, none of the positive feelings she remembered from her encounter with the minister and his wife.

Ellen stopped going to church but she clung to her image of God: "As a child my God was just this very loving person and that's all it was. I liked my Good Shepherd and the lambs."

Ellen's earliest God-image had been formed through the influence of surrogate parents who succeeded in bonding her deeply to themselves. Notice that Ellen did not think of Jesus in the image of Father.

The image she chose correlated with the story of Ellen's personal life. She was, after all, the little lamb lost who had been taken up by a loving pastor. The picture in the Bible spelled out this role dramatically. At the same time Ellen's bonding to her biological parents was very imperfect. She bonded into her surrogate parents and they bonded into her. Thus she was open to their meaning system and began to belong comfortably with them.

The loss of them was traumatic and a further jolt to her slowly forming meaning system. She went through many difficult years growing up but always managed to hold on to her favored image of God. She remained a "lost sheep" even in her own home, feeling that she could not get very close to her parents.

Ellen describes her God-image now in terms of Jesus. "I relate to him as a man who knew human discomforts and problems. I see Jesus as compassionate, very compassionate, a very caring, very forgiving kind of person or God-figure." Feeling that she was not stressing the divine element enough she went on to explain, "I don't mean to say I don't think he is God; it's just that I relate to him more as a very understanding figure, very compassionate."

The cognitive aspect of Ellen's image is Jesus in the form of the Good Shepherd. The non-cognitive aspect is the feeling of being cared for by a compassionate and loving person. God is very real to Ellen but she worships him and relates to him under one favored image. It is this image set into a drama of salvation, the saving of the lost, that informs and enlightens Ellen's LMS.

Ellen's God-image seemed to take a definite form at the tender age of eight. I do not mean to imply that that is usually the case. Nevertheless, children do begin their conceptualizations of God at an early age, and these images reflect not only their communal story but the particularities of their own personalities and the circumstances of their lives. The tailor-made image of God begins its formation early. One image may gain favor in association with a "landmark event" but people are never without their images of God.

Subjective God-Images of Children

A few examples from the work of my graduate students can be enlightening. Let us contrast the drawings of two seven year olds, Penny and Valerie. Both are Roman Catholics.

Penny drew God standing in a garden amid flowers and birds.

When she was asked why she drew him that way she said "I drew him with birds *because I like birds*" (italics mine). "God is smiling because he is happy. There are some birds, flowers, a butterfly on the flowers and a tree. That's the sun in the corner." It all adds up to a pleasant picture by a child with a sunny disposition who loves the outdoors. She lives in the south and has been affected by the nice weather and the woods near her home.

Valerie does not put flowers and birds into her picture. She starts from an entirely different base. Christ is on the cross surrounded by several tearful onlookers. "I drew it like that because it's the first thing I thought about. This is Jesus on the cross. That's Mary and John on one side and Mary Magdalene on the other side. The two women are crying. That's Pontius Pilate at the bottom of the hill. He's not crying because he wanted Jesus to die."

Valerie was amazingly well informed about the people at the cross, probably because her teacher had told the story for Lent. Yet she

Seven-Year-Old Penny's Image of God

remembered names, including Pilate's (which the researcher pronounced from Valerie's efforts).

Even though the scene was sorrowful, Valerie at first put a smile on Jesus' face but then erased it. That is very typical. God is usually smiling in the drawings of children. They assume he is happy—in fact, that he is basically the essence of happiness. Even though we would think Valerie's scene is depressing, for her it was a hero's story in which Jesus was doing something heroic for those around the cross.

The most unusual (and untypical) image of God I have seen was drawn by an eight-year-old girl. God is an older girl in jeans, with two braids and holding balloons. I thought the child misunderstood the question. No, that was her picture of God all right. She said, "God is smiling; *she* has balloons in *her* hand. I was going to draw a lollipop in *her* mouth. *She* sees everything we do" (italics mine).

God is female. I was intrigued by it all, especially the long eyelashes. After some additional questioning I discovered that the little girl

Seven-Year-Old Valerie's Image of God

had drawn her favorite picture—her teenage sister. She did not hesitate to use it when asked to draw a picture of God. The long eyelashes, even though they always go with her "girl" picture, indicate that God "sees everything we do." Bonding to her sister was close, and the picture suggests how easy it is to transfer an image from the home setting into the religious.

Sometimes people ask whether men and women envision God differently. I believe they do. I have noticed, for example, that the drawings of boys and of girls become decidedly different as they get older and the sexual characteristics become more pronounced.

Older boys tend to place God in action, amidst the stars of the heavens, doing something of importance. Girls prefer to concentrate on the personal characteristics of God—holding out his arm, smiling, giving something. The two pictures drawn by twelve-year-olds are fairly typical. The boy says in explanation of his, "God is caring for the troubled world and for all the countries, not just ours. The stars show

Eight Year Old's
Image of God
Drawn as Her Sister

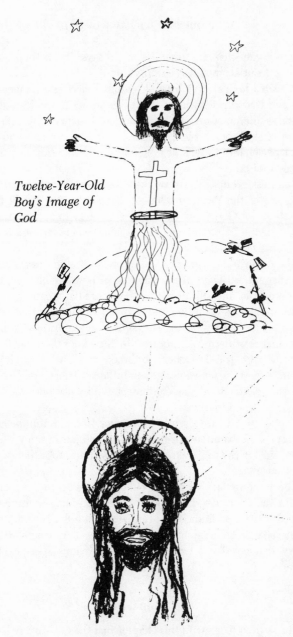

Twelve-Year-Old Boy's Image of God

Twelve-Year-Old Girl's Image of God

that he is bigger than anything." The girl says, "He is the Light of the World, so I put all those rays around him."

It seems logical that their drawings reflect the images in their minds and that this continues as they get older. I would suggest that men and women picture God differently in a manner that reflects their own personal history, which, of course, includes genetics and the specifics of personality as well as the community tradition in which they have been raised.

Feminist groups, aware of the profusion of male images in the story myths of the Western religions, have urged the use of feminine connotations for God. This, of course, is not easy to do because it is not simply a matter of changing "he" to "she" wherever God is referred to in the masculine gender.

The *cognitive* images of God are masculine in most of the story-myths themselves. There is the question of how one changes the story myths in gender and still preserves their essential meaning.

But in the non-cognitive sphere I wonder whether there is a problem at all. The feelings of relatedness to God are distilled at first from the bonding relationships of human life. Men know bonding from their mothers (as well as their fathers) and their wives. Women also know it from their mothers (as well as their fathers). There are, then, at the very basic feeling level, associations of femininity with God already clearly established in our lives.

In other words, we already experience God as feminine in several ways just as we experience a feminine dimension in human bonding. The little girl with her "sister-God" simply dramatizes that perception in her God-image.

The feminists are correct in calling attention to the male dominance in the cognitive dimension of the God-images offered by the Judaeo-Christian tradition. But even with that influence both men and women have been able to find their own dominances, their own imagery that correlates best with their individual personalities and experience.

Summary

I have tried to show in this chapter that the God-image has a central position in every religious LMS. God is proposed as the ultimate reality in the communal stories of the Western religious traditions.

Nevertheless, within the parameters of the general meaning of the word "God" countless individual images are possible. People have favored images which they develop out of the unique circumstances of their lives. Therefore, when the communal story tells its story-myths about God, the individual believer inserts his or her favored image of God, making it possible to feel related to the divine.

The story myths of each faith have two main characters, and the two characters, God and the self, are engaged in very important interactivity. No matter what the story, whether it is Abraham and God or Jesus and God, the *real* religious story lies beneath the characters. It lies with God and me. The story myths of faith and our appropriation of them is the work of our next chapter.

Notes

1. Koran, "Al 'Imran," Chapter 3, Part 3, #60–64.

2. The philosophically oriented work of Ian Ramsey established the value of the model concept in language about God. See his works: *Models and Mystery* (London: Oxford University Press, 1964); *Christian Discourse* (London: Oxford University Press, 1965) and *Words About God* (N.Y.: Harper and Row, 1971) where he puts philosophical and theological language about God into an historical context. See also *Myths, Models and Paradigms* (N.Y.: Harper & Row, 1974). For the use of models as a theological method see Bernard Lonergan, *Method in Theology* (N.Y.: Herder & Herder, 1972), pp. 284–285. An acceptance of the theological pluralism implied in the use of models is evident in David Tracy's *Blessed Rage for Order* (N.Y.: Seabury Press, 1975).

3. Sr. Irene Comeau, S.S.J., "Not Quite Ten Years Later," unpublished Masters thesis, Fairfield University, 1972.

INTEGRATING THE PERSONAL STORY WITH THE COMMUNAL STORY

Chapter Six

The religious tradition of the West has distinguished itself from the religions of the East in the individual distinctiveness of God and in the individuality of humankind. In Judaism, Christianity and Islam, God is clearly separate from man. No matter how benevolent, no matter how compassionate, no matter how deeply involved in human affairs God remains apart from people. Religion in the West is a matter of the quality of the relationship between two identities, between two clearly separate and defined individuals, God and man.

In the East, man and the divine are organically related. Man finds the peace and bliss of divinity within itself, usually by stripping away falseness and diverting desires. Man, God and the world of nature are not related to each other externally, in interaction but organically and interiorly.

Thus, in the East people must locate their place in the unfolding creation, fit into their social position, perform the duties expected of them as part of the role they play within the living whole of all things. Individual choices and personal decisions are minimized in the face of the larger task, assuming the part accorded to people by the structure of the divine which is within all things.

Choice in Western Religious Belief

The Western stress on the individual who makes a difference can be found as early as the eighth century Hebrew prophets. The prophets tell the people that responsible conduct and repentance cause God to change. God will turn from his momentary wrath and return to his more normal condition of enduring love in the face of genuine repentance. The responsible conduct of kings and peoples can actually affect the all-important relationship between God and humankind. That, of course, is never the case in the East where people are never so important as to disturb the unfolding divine activity taking place within all things.

As the years proceed in Western civilization the emphasis on individuality and personhood deepens. With the advent of Christianity it extends into the inner person, the inner reaches of the self, his or her most personal feelings and thoughts. The self is indeed sacred, not with the sanctity of the divine as in the East, but sanctified by its origins, its relationship to the divine, by its own autonomy, its own freedom, its ability to choose. And that God-given ability to choose is so basic, so essential, that it extends even to the possibility of choosing or not choosing God.

As a result of this heritage our present Western society has heartily approved the uniqueness of people, their once-for-all character. Since each life will be lived only once and is unrepeatable, the quality of that life is important. Death must be held at bay for as long as possible.

Creative thought and works are praised as reflections of individuality. Each person has his or her own precious story which is the account of how that person met the challenge of individuality.

Because people in the West are convinced that they are free by divine decree, they feel good about exercising that freedom. Parents teach their children very early that they must grow in the exercise of freedom. Later they must be prepared to choose a college, a career, a spouse, the life that will bring them fulfillment.

The dynamics of choice pervade the entire realm of religious experience in Western thought and life. Subtly people enter into the process of not only choosing God but choosing the *kind* of God that will influence their lives. This is a profoundly important truth for the religious educator to understand. Not only is there a possible choice, for or against God. There is also the choice of the kind of God, the form under which God will be known, as a central influence in one's life. Each person arrives at a unique perception of God which is special to him or her.

Some may object that our Christian and Jewish faiths give us no such permission. Nowhere is it written down, nowhere is it preached, that people can pick and choose, select and discard what is appropriate for them in their religious tradition.

Permission is given quite clearly, however, as part of the very fabric of education in the West. It begins as early as kindergarten when individuality of expression, even in the crudest artwork, is praised. Every crayon drawing, every model constructed, every clay figure that has an element of individual creativity is praised. Children are encouraged to think for themselves, to stand apart in what they do. Very early they are led to select their own toys, their own books, their own clothes, and, when it comes to high school and college, even their own paths of education.

Selection and choice are bred into our perception of individual personhood, a perception not stressed in Eastern religious thought. Selection and choice are integral to religious development because God and humankind are conceptualized as entities totally and entirely separate from each other. God is understood as choosing people. People are conceived of as responding to God. God extends his arms in the first overture of love; people accept and complete the circle of relatedness.

This is where the human experience of bonding becomes so important. The choice of the specific God-image within the structure of a particular story-myth is not a cold, calculating, intellectual decision. To perceive it that way would be to entirely misconstrue the phenomenon.

Choice as a Loving Response

The choice of "one's God" within a story-myth is an emotional choice. It is a matter of feeling, of fidelity, of love. The bonding capacity, the capacity for love that has been learned and nourished in childhood, is brought into the selection. Relating to one's God is a matter of *loving* choice.

The entire process is clearly analogous to the Western understanding of love and marriage. We believe that selecting a marriage partner is an entirely free choice, yet it is a loving choice. Each person wants to see his or her love given freely. Yet each wants to feel loved as well. The school of learning about love, understood in this way, is the home. The home is where bonding is learned. The child experiences love and responds to it. The believer experiences love, the love of God, and responds to it. The base of religious experience in the West is not loving; it is *being loved*. That is the starting point in the divine-human relational process.

Prayer expresses the character of this relationship, particularly prayers that are spontaneously formulated. Examining our prayer patterns will help us understand our preferred God-image. Often enough, it will help us beyond that, to an indication of the story-myth which helps to make our God-image functional.

A good example of freely formulated prayers revealing a God-image is presented to us in the writings of the celebrated Christian saint and scholar, Augustine of Hippo. His writing style mingles prayers to God with his reflections and theological insights. If we study the *Confessions* we will get a clear picture of the kind of prayer that was his at this period in his life and thus gain entry into his preferred God-image, as well as his favored story-myth. We will discover how he actually had a part in choosing his own God-image.

At the very beginning of the *Confessions* (Book One, Chapter 4) Augustine addresses *his* God and thereby reveals his favored God-image:

O Highest, Best, most Powerful, most Omnipotent, most Merciful and most Just, most Hidden and most Evident, most Beautiful and most Strong, Stable and Incomprehensible, Immutable; moving all things, never new, never old, renewing all things; 'bringing the proud to senility and they know it not'; ever active, ever quiet, gathering in and requiring nothing, perfecting, seeking, when nothing is lacking to Thee. Thou lovest, but art not disturbed by passion; Thou art jealous, but free from care; Thou art repentant, but not sorrowful; Thou art angry, but calm; Thou changest Thy words, but not Thy plan; Thou dost recover what Thou findest, but has never lost; never in need, Thou dost rejoice in gain; never covetous, Thou dost demand payment with interest. More than Thou askest is given Thee, so that Thou mayest be in debt, but who has anything which is not Thine? Thou payest debts while owing no one; remittest debts while losing nothing. What have we said, my God, my Life, my holy Sweetness—or what can anyone say— when he speaks of Thee? Yet, woe to those who do not speak of Thee; for though they talk much, they say nothing.[1]

At first glance it seems that almost every quality tumbles from Augustine's lips in praise of his God. But what comes first are qualities from philosophical categories that reflect his personal background. God is the highest good; he is most just but, at the same time, most merciful. That, in capsule, is the story of Augustine's life. God is omnipotent and changeless but the renewer of all things. Augustine is the one renewed by this awesome power. His prayer is an interweaving of images taken from (1) his philosophical past along with images gleaned from (2) the Old Testament, a God who can be jealous and a God who can repent. The paradoxes of belief are stressed, balancing the changeless God of the philosophers against the intensely committed God of Scripture.

Surprising as it is, Augustine's dominant God-image is not Jesus. His God is the loving, immutable One who fills Augustine with all good things, who has loved him intensely, who has renewed his life and who now serves as his enlightenment. This highest Good is worthy of Augustine's most central interest and efforts. He knows from experience that his heart will find no rest until it rests in him (*Confessions*, Book One, Chapter I). Augustine's future rests in his secure bonding to his loving God.

There is a dominant story-myth which informs Augustine's life and it does not correlate closely with any one specific Gospel story. Yet it does capture the sentiments presented in the New Testament, especially in Paul, of a "saving, regenerating God." I propose that "what is happening" for Augustine is that the all-powerful, immutable One suffuses the within of people with the renewing power of love. It is a strong, almost overpowering action, yet many do not recognize it in their lives as Augustine himself did not during his dissolute youth.

He sees many people seeking themselves or even seeking God in the "without" of things, in external affairs. But God presents himself to the "within" of people who have only to acknowledge and accept the interior stirrings. Augustine learned this from his own personal story. It worked powerfully for him and changed his entire life. It is now his central perception which he offers to his readers as an interpretation of God's activity in the world.

In the *conversion* experience God spoke *directly* to Augustine through the words of Paul, "Let us behave with decency as befits the day: no reveling or drunkenness, no debauchery or vice, no quarrels or jealousies! Let Christ Jesus himself be the armor that you wear: give no more thought to satisfying the bodily appetites" (Rom 13:13).

For the first time Augustine heard these words directed to him personally; he heard them as an *insider*. It was a moment of intense emotion that brought him to tears. In an instant of clarity he was able to see himself as an ungrateful recipient of countless blessings, and thus the object of immense divine love.

The enlightenment struck with overpowering clarity, coming from *outside the self*. It was a disclosure that the self did not bring about. In Western thought God is the source of this disclosure. It is recognized as the force of divine grace which, like a light, shines upon the self, clarifying one's personal story.

Here we have a thumbnail sketch depicting a dramatic moment in one person's coming to faith. Augustine, in his personal story, had already developed a God-image, long before his conversion. This was the image from philosophy combined with imagery from the Old Testament. The moment of faith came as a gift when he realized how deeply he was loved by his God. And this story, of a God lovingly generous to his creatures, is part of the communal story that Augustine had heard many times before but *as an outsider*. In this moment God spoke to him directly. Augustine heard it *as an insider*.

I am proposing that Augustine's God-image, formed largely through his own choices, did not change in conversion. But in the grace-filled moment that view of God was understood as profoundly correct and addressing him personally and directly. Augustine had a "now" God to whom he was emotionally bonded. He also had a story in which to situate the activity of his God.

His entire life changed dramatically. A new meaning system had become established sending repercussions throughout his whole approach to life. His work as a rhetorician was abandoned, his pursuit of honor transformed, his common-law wife dismissed. The new LMS called for a complete reorientation of the self.

Let us now turn to another kind of example. It is taken from the very pages of Sacred Scripture itself. In this example, we see how a conceptualization of Jesus, viewed as of ultimate importance, fits together with a story-myth that gives intense meaning to the life of the writer—and to countless others who have read it.

Integration in the Gospel Itself

At the beginning of the Gospel according to Luke in the New Testament we are presented with a scene in which Jesus preaches his first sermon in the synagogue in his home town of Nazareth. Two other evangelists, Matthew and Mark, record a similar event but they do not report the content of Jesus' sermon.

Luke presents Jesus reading from the scroll of Isaiah and announcing clearly the purpose of his ministry:

> The spirit of the Lord is upon me because he has anointed me; he has sent me to announce good news to the poor, to proclaim release for prisoners and recovery of sight for the blind; to let the broken victims go free, to proclaim the year of the Lord's favor (Lk 4:16f).

In this account Jesus is portrayed identifying himself as the saver of the lost. The incident serves as the frontispiece of the entire Gospel, striking the first note of a theme that will occur again and again throughout the Gospel.

The Jesus-image that Luke prefers and has recaptured for his community is the Jesus who saves Gentiles as well as Jews, the poor as well as the rich, women as well as men.

While the theme of a saving Jesus is also present in the Gospels of Mark and Matthew, it is not the single focusing center of these works as it is for Luke. Mark and Matthew both have their own emphases which correspond with their perception of the identity and mission of Jesus. Here I stress the important contribution of Luke and, in fact, of each evangelist as they reframe the meaning and ministry of Jesus for their own personal contexts.

Luke proposes to the listeners of his Gospel that they understand Jesus *primarily* as Savior and follow in his saving ministry. This rather clear understanding of what Jesus was about in his lifetime and what the Christian ought to be about, I suggest, we call Luke's dominant religious story-myth, the integrating focus of his religious life.

For Luke, the story of God effecting the salvation of humankind through Jesus is the most important fact in all of human life. To paraphrase Paul Tillich, it is the meaning that gives meaning to all other meanings. Luke tells the story as an "insider," as one emotionally committed to his faith, as one with a deep bonding toward Jesus.

With this perception of reality in place the evangelist has a base upon which to structure his entire meaning system. He can commit himself and invite the commitment of others around this organizing principle.

The dominant religious story-myth joins together the isolated religious appropriations of one's previous life into a single structure of meaning. It does not answer every question or solve every problem by any means. It does, however, provide the internal organizational focus upon which one can build meaning. This meaning supplies governance for the LMS. Luke did not make up the conceptualization of Jesus as liberator. It was already in the communal story that he received. When he grasped this dimension of the Jesus story, however, it clicked for him and became the key to meaning around which everything else fell into place.

The dominant story-myth has to correspond with the personal story. It receives priority of place because the events of a person's life have prepared him or her to appreciate this specific story. The impressive events and the landmark experiences of life (along with the basic personality structure) have helped to shape an awareness of the self. It is this special awareness of the self that finds particular story-myths more meaningful than any others. Most of the time the influence of a story-myth is subtle. Its selection is not a momentous, deliberate act. It is like an all-pervading mist, soft and penetrating, never bulky or obvious. For those persons who have experienced an integration of their life the central story-myth explains what human life is about and what their role is in relation to the divine story.

Integration Is Highly Personalized

While each religious faith tradition has its own central story-myth, that particular story may *not* form the organizing center of the believer's meaning system. Christianity, for example, sets the story of the passion and resurrection of Jesus at the center of its religious message. That does not mean that each individual Christian holds this story as central. In actual practice, it appears, as in Augustine's case, that the *personal* story is more influential in determining God-images and central story-myths than is the communal story.

The cases of two or our interviewees would seem to bear this out. Dan, a forty-two-year-old Roman Catholic, the father of three children, achieved an integration in his life which is very much like that presented to us by the Gospel of Luke. For Dan, his central story-myth incorporates Jesus as the sole meaningful God-image. God is known in a practical way only in the form of Jesus. Dan is not much concerned with God the Father, nor with the Holy Spirit. The activity that Jesus as God is engaged in is the ministry of helping people. That is what Jesus did in his lifetime; he cured people, made them feel better. That is what he does now.

Dan sees himself here on earth to do as Jesus did—to help others. When the opportunity arose for him to prepare for ordination to become a deacon in the Catholic Church, he jumped at it.

Now ordained, he views his ministry as a kind of partnership with Jesus. He is now helping Jesus in the service of other people. He has a special gift for working with the elderly and the sick in his parish. This ministry provides the central motivation for his life. While his regular job is still important to him, he says that he thinks he could lose it without being profoundly shaken. But he would not want to lose his ministry.

Dan's basic orientation correlates his personal self-perception as a friendly, helping person with the story-myth of Jesus as the saver of the unfortunate. His integration lies there. Jesus as Savior in the imagery of the cross is not central to his consciousness. If a spiritual counselor were to work with Dan, he or she might point out this basic orientation and how closely it follows the approach of Luke's Gospel. Dan's readings and prayerful reflections might be nourished from that Gospel and further religious "reappropriations" could take place around the basic story-myth of Jesus as the saver of others.

Contrast Dan with another Christian, Harley, a thirty-three-year-old, brought up in the Methodist tradition. Harley, like Dan, does not see Jesus in his sufferings as central. Harley told us that religion was never particularly important in his life when he was growing up. He spent his youth worrying about his inadequacies. As the last of five children he always had the impression that he was not important, even not wanted. By the time he was into his twenties he had become deeply involved with drugs.

At twenty-eight, disgusted with himself, he sought out a drug counselor entirely on his own. The counselor worked with him to improve his self-image, taught him how to affirm and to assert himself, to speak up for his rights and to say what he thought. Harley gained confidence not only in his opinions but in his strengths and eventually freed himself of the drug habit.

Religion entered Harley's life in a real way during his rehabilitation when he learned to pray. In prayer he applied the same methods that worked for him in social situations. He told God just what he was thinking—no pious phrases, no "pulling of punches." His prayer was almost confrontational.

God was the one who encouraged, even challenged Harley to say exactly what he felt. God would hold him responsible for his conduct, but nothing truly devastating could happen to him if he remained honest with God. God was (and is) Harley's support, the one upon whom he can rely totally. This is his point of integration. This relationship to God supplies central meaning to his life, keeps him away from the world of drugs and helps him to function with greater self-confidence.

In analyzing Harley's personal story we suspect that he was not bonded very deeply to start with. He sensed this as a child. Consequently he was not bonded into the religious tradition of his parents. There was no strong communal tradition from which to draw a story-myth. When he finally came to an awareness of his problem, grasped the root causes that were making his life miserable, he was able to see himself correctly. Integration then became a possibility.

Through prayer Harley was able to envision the divine as a "now" God with a "now" reality. God (not as Jesus) is the support of people. Thus, his story-myth—God is our everyday strength and support—comes in a general way from his Christian tradition but is strongly influenced by his own *personal* story with his own deep personal needs. Although Harley is a prayerful Christian and his relationship to God gives great meaning to his life, most of the aspects of the Christian teaching, including addressing prayer to Christ, are not part of his ordinary and daily experience. The story of the passion and resurrection of Christ, objectively central to Christianity, and, it would seem, perfectly apropos for his own life's story, does not appeal to him or grip the center of his consciousness.

The Roots of Integration

Sometimes it seems possible to trace the *origins* of a person's God-image and from the unique circumstances of that person's life-story to see how the dominant story-myth is arrived at and the God-image fits in.

That appears to be the case with Anna, a Cuban woman in her late thirties. In her interviews, Anna spoke of her "sweet and gentle Christ" as the constant companion in her life to whom she prays frequently during the day.

She turns to her Christ as a friend with the feeling that he will always take care of her. Anna, now divorced, and the mother of three, has many concerns and difficulties.

It is Christ, as a divine person, with whom she shares the drama of her interior life. Christ and she live out each day together perhaps in a conceptualization that might best be described symbolically as marriage.

Christ is Anna's Savior but not in his death and resurrection long ago. He is her Savior "now" in the form of the still living Christ, her companion in life. Starting with the basic story of salvation she has adapted it to her own specific needs.

Let me now tie-in Anna's "marriage metaphor" with what I said in the previous chapter. The God-image in Anna's God-man relationship is Christ. But what are the specific characteristics of this God-image, this Christ? He is "sweet and gentle."

Where did she get the idea that he is sweet and gentle? Has she extracted it from her experience with her father? No, he was quite the opposite. She felt little warmth toward her father. She described him as demanding and sometimes abusive.

Anna selectively borrowed from the Gospels. I say selectively because she obviously skipped over the scene in which Christ casts the money-changers out of the temple but perhaps preferred Christ with the little children. I think, however, that she was predisposed to do this because of her *mother* who was her favored parent and whom she described as "soft-spoken and gentle." It was her mother with whom she made the deepest religious associations. Her mother attended church faithfully and kept many religious objects in the home. But, most significantly, it was her mother to whom she was deeply bonded.

The notion of Christ as "sweet and gentle" is a composite drawn from selected images of Christ found in the Gospels along with the experiences of her mother's gentle personality embedded in her consciousness through deep bonding.

The conceptualization of Christ (cognitive dimension) and her relatedness to Christ (non-cognitive) is a blend of thoughts and feelings supplied by the community tradition (Christianity) and by her close bonding to her favored parent (her mother).

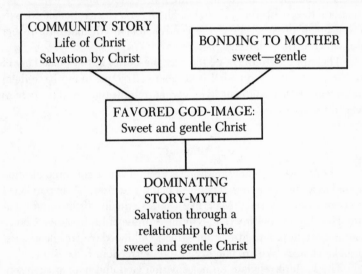

The story-myth of the redemption of Christ has been told and retold for centuries by the Church. It is recorded in its changeless scriptural form. But it is subjectively colored and contoured by individuals, used pragmatically in various forms to sustain the framework of different people's meaning systems.

Given each story-myth, some elements are subjectively suppressed, others are emphasized. For Anna, Christ's physical sufferings do not help to give any rationale to contemporary human suffering. She confided that she is often disturbed by TV news reports of events where people are shown undergoing terrible suffering. It triggers memories of her own sufferings and those of her family members and friends back in her country.

Her problem: How can a loving Christ permit such terrible things in the world? Why does he permit it to continue?

When asked, "How do you react to these thoughts?" she said, "I put them out of my mind. I don't like to think about it."

Anna flees a confrontation with ideas that would threaten her LMS. Her favored image of God and her marriage-like relationship to Christ are too precious to lose, too highly endowed with life-meaning to risk. To view Christ as punishing or cruel or insensitive to human misery would be to shatter her faith and her meaning system. So she sets aside these disturbing thoughts. She has no clear rationale for suffering but it does not affect the central story-myth that informs her life, which is the "marriage metaphor."

That appears to me to be the way the stories of faith take hold of us. We draw from them what is uniquely attractive to us, shape them and integrate them into our lives, giving rich meaning and purpose to everything we do.

Summary

The Western religious tradition is grounded in a conceptualization of God as a unique, personal being, a being who exercises unparalleled freedom in his decisions. Man, like God, is equally distinct and separate. His ultimate destiny resides in the exercise of his freedom. Choice is an important part of life. From earliest childhood we are encouraged to make choices. We are taught to exercise freedom responsibly.

The Eastern religions do not envision God and man as such separate entities nor do they concern themselves with the importance of a relationship between God and humankind. Buddha thought that the idea of God was a distraction, and the millions of Hindu gods are more like the patron saints in Christianity than like an ultimate reality. Choice and decision-making are not crucial; acceptance, interior oneness and freedom from concern are far more significant for the religious life.

The dynamics of religious appropriation must then function within the parameters of the structures of reality as perceived separately in Eastern and Western religious thought.

Thus, the West places enormous importance on each individual life. Consequently the personal story looms into great significance in the Western consciousness. Impressive events and landmark experiences are dramatic turning points in the all-important personal story. Pragmatically then, the pressure is on the individual to place himself or herself into the center of the spotlight, the position of ultimate importance.

One arrives at a God-image early in life, constructed by the self primarily out of the experiences of one's personal story. (I cannot imagine a Buddhist child undergoing the same experience.) The image of God requires a field of action, an appropriate story-myth, one that appeals to the events of one's life history.

Prayer is an important clue to helping people determine the way they perceive God. If the content of freely formulated prayers is analyzed one can discover one's preferred God-image and, quite often, the prevailing story-myth in which it functions.

Story-myths abound in the community religious tradition, but it does not follow that what is central for the tradition will be a central story for the individual.

It is when one begins to hear the favored story as an insider, directed personally and individually to the self, with one's own God-image fitting into place, that religious integration occurs. This is a dramatic development for the religious life of a person in the Western religions. This story, "what is happening" between God and people, begins to govern the meaning in one's life, becomes the center of direction and motivation. All things then become possible because a genuine truth about life is appreciated. In fact, for the religious self, *the* truth around which all life is centered has been found. Appreciating that truth is not simply an intellectual insight; it is suffused with love. It is a process in which the self has often perceived itself as gifted, graced, and has made a choice, accepted the overture. The self is bonded to God in a distinctly new way.

Note

1. *The Fathers of the Church: St. Augustine, Confessions,* trans. by Vernon J. Bourke (N.Y.: Fathers of the Church, Inc., 1953), p. 6.

THE PATH TO INTEGRATION

Chapter Seven

Personal integration is a high point of religious development. It is not the pinnacle but it does represent a decisive framing of the structure of meaning. From there, the person is prepared to move on to greater heights, to appreciate myth at a second level of consciousness, to grow in religious faith.

People come to religious integration slowly, that is, through a life-growth process that prepares them for it. I hesitate to call the process a series of stages[1] because I do not find them so distinct or irreversible. I am more comfortable with an overlapping process, a matter of perceptual patterns that seem to be transformed as new personal experiences are correlated with one's religious tradition.

Symbolic Acceptance

We have already established the central importance of bonding in infancy and early childhood. If bonded successfully a child finds meaning within the context of loving parents. The acts of caring along with the child's developing self-growth provide the very first bases for meaning.

All the religious faiths of the world, East or West, are initially shared through bonding. All the children of this world learn their basic religious identification through bonding. This is the way they become insiders and belongers.

The acceptance of symbols, stories, songs and rituals is not primarily an intellectual process. It is emotional, tied to love, a dimension of parental affection. Symbolic acceptance is the very first step in religious development.

The symbols that a child accepts uncritically are the prayers, practices, patterns and images of his or her parents' faith. These are not cohesively linked or coordinated in the child's mind. They are simply held together by the affective glue of parental bonding.

No reasons are necessary to belong to the faith of one's parents. One belongs because one is securely attached to them. This attachment makes each child an "insider" within the parental faith tradition.

Parents give a name to the many symbols and practices that constitute the child's religious heritage. Naming puts together a host of isolated practices: "We are Catholics," "We are Episcopalians," "We are Jews."

A conversation overheard recently by a Jewish mother is very typical of life in the United States where the children of different faith communities play with each other. Maryanne, a Catholic child, eight years old, said to Judy, the daughter of the Jewish woman, "I am going to get a bike for Christmas." Judy answered, "Good, then we can ride our bikes together when it gets warmer." As an afterthought Judy added, "We don't have Christmas; we have Hannukah."

The conversation ended there. Each little girl accepted her own religious designation rather happily and without question. If you are a Catholic, you have Christmas. If you are a Jew, you have Hannukah. Neither one wants the other's holidays any more than they want the other's parents. They take for granted what is and what is not part of their heritage.

While symbolic acceptance is predominantly a perception of childhood, it seems to continue throughout life. Adults will accept symbols and new rituals without criticism when presented to them by authorities within their faith tradition. The elderly in the Episcopal and Roman Catholic faiths are now experiencing new rituals and blessings for the sick in prayer and healing services. They accept these in the trusted contexts of their parish churches and from the hands of their parish priests.

Surely not all adults accept innovation so gracefully but those who do, who have been long bonded to their tradition, indicate how an attitude of symbolic acceptance can continue throughout life.

Symbolic acceptance as a dominant perception in childhood gives way to a new dominance when individuality and personal decision making begins to gain entrance into the consciousness.

As I mentioned earlier, personal decision making is heartily approved in our Western culture—and the earlier the better. Parents praise their enterprising little daughters who go out and get a paper route and spend their earnings on things they want. Little boys who start their own "businesses" of recycling paper or collecting returnable bottles are encouraged and congratulated.

Personal Appropriation

When individual choice enters into religious affiliation I see this as part of a pattern I call "personal appropriation." Personal appropriation is the unique appreciation of a *favored* image, story or ritual, even a song that resonates sympathetically with one's view of oneself.

Very early in life, as I have already shown, children begin formulating their personal God-image, and this God-image is consistent with the particularities of their own personal story. In an earlier example I showed Ellen, the young child taken in by a Presbyterian minister and his wife, as appropriating an image of God in the form of Jesus, the Good Shepherd. She carried that image into adulthood.

In addition to the God-image, children filter out favorite stories, favorite parts of a religious service, favorite hymns, favorite prayers. Nine-year-old Jimmy is a very active and aggressive boy who likes electronic war games, bombs and guns. He has been exposed to a lot of bible stories but David and Goliath is one of his favorites. He likes the part about the slingshot. This is only one "personal appropriation" out of many. There are other factors that affect other personal appropriations, the kinds of attitudes stressed in his home, the kind of God-image taking form in his mind, the kinds of prayers he says and the occasions on which he learns to say them. At Jimmy's age there is no one integrating principle which organizes these varied personal appropriations into a single, meaningful whole.

Often enough the personal appropriation has a negative dimension, that is, something is rejected. This is sometimes upsetting for parents but because the rejection or criticism is rendered as an "insider" the attitude is not too disturbing.

Here is the way personal appropriation may look from the negative point of view. Neil is eleven and a very bright little boy. He surprised his confirmation teacher by telling her he was not ready for a "commitment to Christ," the theme of the confirmation class. None of the other children thought of that, or if they did they kept quiet about it.

Neil's father (a philosophy professor) liked the way his son spoke up for himself, so he arranged with the teacher to have Neil excused for another year. Neil was rewarded for his expression of individuality. The reward reinforces his attitude toward personal decision making.

If we ask a class of sixth graders to describe their favorite Bible story we will get a variety of choices based on what appealed to each one of them. Personal appropriation is rooted in the experiences of the self and the structure of one's personality.

As adolescence arrives slowly in its silent, almost imperceptible way, the symbols and stories of faith that have been personally appropriated begin to be related to each other. I do not see this as a stage, but merely as an ongoing development that is taking place in other areas of the child's mind. Relationships are being made; connections and associations try to organize the piecemeal appropriations of the earlier years.

Examples of this are quite ordinary. Ronnie, a fourteen-year-old Catholic boy, put together his musical interest along with the personal appropriations of his religious faith. One Sunday he was invited to bring his guitar to a folk Mass which was held in another local parish. The people gathered around a temporary altar in the parish hall. The music was loud and lively and the young people thoroughly enjoyed themselves.

When Ronnie got home he told his parents he had joined the folk group and was not going to attend Mass at his home parish anymore. He used the occasion to say that he never liked his parish church very much anyway. "It was a drag going there."

Ronnie did not risk much. He had a sense that his parents would let him do what he wanted. Actually they were just as happy that he had suddenly become excited about going to church.

It was more of a problem for the parents of a sixteen-year-old Jewish boy. One day he began putting masking tape across the edge of the refrigerator door to prevent it from opening. Every time his parents went to the refrigerator to get something they had to tear through another strand of tape. Finally there was a family showdown.

Morris had been protesting the kind of food his parents kept in the refrigerator. His rationale was simple: If they were Jews, why didn't they do what they were supposed to do? Foods that are not permitted are clearly written down in the Torah. They know what is not permitted; why didn't they observe it? It was an argument presented to him by one of his orthodox friends and it made sense.

The dietary laws constituted a single issue, but it was pushing on to a question that had more far-reaching, global ramifications. How observant was he going to be in the practice of his Jewish faith?

At sixteen Morris was looking at the issue in black and white terms. It is either right or wrong to eat food proscribed by the law. If it is wrong, why do it? He had put together several separate appropriations and his faith began to take on new meaning.

The rigid, right or wrong stance, I believe, is part of a healthy religious development.[2] To the person who experiences religious conviction in these terms it is an advance over the inherited, less passionate position of a previous stance. One's faith begins to take on a new seriousness with new possibilites unfolding.

For the adolescent like Morris who arrives at a right or wrong stance, the outcome is consummated in very practical terms, in terms of doing something. It is not speculative. Personal appropriation always proceeds from acts of individuality to associations and linkages and then finally to central meanings.

Parents are the first ones to feel the stings of personal appropriation as new connections are made. Notice how both Ronnie and Morris looked for feedback from their parents and bounced their feelings and opinions off them, inviting a response. Because of bonding, parents are very much still a part of the personal revolution that goes on within their children. Bonding leads the child to ask, "What do my parents think about this? What will they say?" The adolescent lays down what sounds like an infallible pronouncement but it is really a question. What comes out as "I'm not going to church anymore" means "Why do I keep going to church? What does it do for me?"

There is rejection in "appropriation," rejection of specific practices, rejection of ways of thinking. But this rejection, necessary as it is for individualization, goes on from within the tradition during adolescence when bonding has been secure. Adolescents, bound into the tradition through their parents, will not break through to a position so new that they become outsiders.

It is my contention that adolescents who *do* become outsiders to their nurturing tradition, who leave the faith of their parents and become members of another religion, suffered bonding problems in their earlier years. In making a strong statement like this I imply that parents who are committed to their faith tradition and have established strong emotional bonds with their children will not witness these children breaking out of their religion while they are adolescents.

But even though children so bonded do not break with their tradition, they are still capable of individualizing their heritage and appropriating their faith in giant steps. They are not silent replicas, clones of their parents' faith. They have their own lives, their own range of experiences, their own impressive events that give shape to their religious faith in new ways.

Myth Embodied in Living Models

To the onlooking parent the intuitive understanding of myth that sparkled throughout earlier childhood seems to be temporarily out of order in adolescence. The interest in superheroes, fueled by TV and comic books in the pre-teen years, seems gone.

Logic seems to have come into power and everything is subjected to its rigid scrutinies. The practices and beliefs of faith are no exception. The mythical character of religious stories is not appreciated when elbowed out by a new historical consciousness. "If it didn't happen, what's the sense of talking about it? It isn't real." Reality, understood as what is happening, is more important.

Myth, however, in adolescence, is by no means dead. And it is still the bearer of meaning but clothed in new form. Myth is now embodied in the lives of real people. If we recall the three dimensions of myth that I spoke of earlier, the visual image, the "now" character and the emotional relationship, we will see them still present.

The visual image is replaced by the living person, the rock star, the tennis pro, the fashion model, the research scientist. The image now exists in imitable flesh-and-blood. That accounts for the importance of personal appearances in the lives of adolescents. They want to see the rock star, see the tennis pro for themselves, sometimes even touch him, in an effort to get closer to that reality.

This seeing and touching is an intensification of the "now" character of myth. The flesh and blood hero gives a "new" reality to the idea of personal success. It is real and "unreal" at the same time. There is truth to their success stories and there is plenty of media "hype" in it as well—and the adolescents realize it. But it is food for the imagination, for inspiration, for a better future.

There is also a bonding to the heroes, a collecting of their pictures, a romantic listening to their records, a following of them to their performances. The devotee is *affiliated* to the hero.

The personal appropriations of adolescence, therefore, still include the appreciation for myth. But myth lives on in real heroes, persons one can read about in the papers, see on TV or in person.

Real life *religious* heroes can have enormous impact on the meaning system of an adolescent under the same rubrics. The adolescent is fascinated by the religiously motivated adult who serves as a model for the faith the teenager has inherited.

It is interesting, for example, that the religious order started by Mother Teresa of Calcutta to care for the poor of India gains new followers among the young every day while the older orders find practically no new candidates. She is a flesh-and-blood embodiment of the Christian ideal of charity and therefore serves as a real model "now." That physical presence is an essential supplement to the theoretical ideal of Christianity that is taught out of books. Adolescents need to see people "doing it" to give verification to their ideals.

Role models outside the family are part of the expanding circle of experience that opens up in adolescence and young adulthood. Adults who are attractive to young people are surrogate parents in the wider world of experience. Adolescents would like to bond to them. This is how "disciples" are generated. Young disciples are bound to God through the mediatorship of their real life role model.

As Jean Piaget instructs us about adolescence, it is the time in which formal operational thinking comes into full blossom. The adolescent exercises this thinking on the subject of his or her faith. But the reflection is not a careful, studied pondering of the logic of the entire system of faith. It is, rather, a passing over the same beliefs, many times, from many different directions. It is a kind of cyclic review of the story-myths of faith, of their truths, from the vantage points of day-to-day experience. When, therefore, an adult comes along who is the embodiment of what the young person has learned theoretically, that adult is powerfully appealing. Further, when the adult can articulate his or her vision of faith, smooth out the intellectual conflicts, make faith come alive and seem eminently possible, then the adolescent has a genuine faith-sharer. Here is the disciple-master, bonding relationship that is so helpful to religious growth.

Early Commitment

The period in a young person's life between the ages of about eighteen to twenty-one is a prime time for a certain kind of religious commitment highly influenced by role models and serious intellectual reflection on one's inherited faith. At this time a young person is capable of making a serious and full-fledged commitment. While the generosity and self-giving of this commitment cannot be questioned, there is still a "global perception," a certain unity of faith that is not yet possible at this age.

What I am suggesting is that the young person has not processed enough experiential data in life to construct a LMS that can bear the weight of the systems-wide need.

The role model's ideological faith system has been taken on but it must now be tested in the stress situations that arise in the twenties. The sobering stresses of the world of work and of loving relationships put their pressure on the structures of this meaning system. One of the most powerful tests to the meaning system will be the meaning systems of others, particularly others to whom the young person may be emotionally attracted. Only after negotiating these challenging experiences will the young person be ready to cap the structure, integrate his or her faith-life, solidify a strong LMS.

When young idealistic persons who made a serious faith commitment between eighteen and twenty-one arrive at the end of their twenties they will discover a need for a "deeper commitment," a new dedication of the self, which, looking back on the earlier one, they now see as tentative and incomplete. It is at this time that integration can take place. The personal story has logged enough experience to have a good grasp of one's own real identity.

Later Commitment Through Integration

The religious tradition, the one uncritically accepted in early childhood, then personally appropriated in piecemeal fashion, then appropriated with connections and associations, has been pretty well scrutinized. Its strengths are known as well as its weaknesses. All have coalesced around a central understanding, a story-myth that explains life meaning with power. It is fully worthy of leading to God (in the West), a rationale that can set prayer into place. Thus a deep, life-directing commitment is now possible.

In the Christian and Jewish traditions the possibility of that commitment is understood as suffused with God's initiating overtures of love. When that is the case, the commitment is consummated.

That is what happened to Paul of Tarsus and that is what happened to Augustine of Hippo as I mentioned in the previous chapter. We do not know Paul's age at the time of his conversion but we do know that Augustine was thirty-three years old.

The early thirties is a time for serious decision making in Western religious practice. It seems that a person needs the life experience of the twenties, needs time to reflect on these experiences, to scrutinize the heritage of faith in order to be prepared for the kind of consolidation and stabilization of the LMS that commitment produces. When Martin Luther took the step of nailing his ninety-five theses to the church door at Wittenberg he was thirty-two years old. He could not have done that five years earlier in his life.

For most people religious integration is less dramatic than Paul's or Augustine's but the results are *equally less* dramatic. Lives are not turned around dramatically, but a solidification of the meaning system is reached so that the religiously motivated person is able to progress to new levels of understanding and appreciation within faith.

The person who has reached a personal religious integration may be seen by others as one who "has it all together." It is not so simple or all together as it seems, but, by comparison, others, onlookers, see the integrated person as having a religious centering that is not knocked off course by the shocks and jolts of life. The integrated person, first and foremost, seems to have a vision of reality, clearly perceived. This vision is centered around a faith story that serves as the organizer of all the other myths that are operative in a person's life.

This central and organizing myth captures the heart of one's self-conceptualization as well as the heart of the mythology of one's religious tradition as one has come to understand it. Once securely established, it forms the central structure of the life meaning system (LMS).

Reappropriation

The religiously mature person continues to grow in faith experience throughout life. After integration the pattern is one of *reappropriation*, that is, a second level of appreciation for the story-myths and symbols of one's faith.

In a lifetime, people who have set their objective as relating to the divine hear the same truths repeated many times. In each of these cyclic renewals new depths of richness and of meaning can be drawn from the same materials. Each journey over the familiar ground yields new awarenesses.

Myth survives the rational scrutinies of young adulthood and becomes a rich mine of new meanings as the older person pours into its interpretation the wealth of life experience that has been amassed.

The Genesis story of man's fall, for example, and the divine love that ever stands ready to welcome him back is a classic myth that never dies. As the personal story of each individual piles up experience the self sees how much of Adam is in him or her. The story is truly a description of the dynamics in the life of the self. The sequel of God's enduring love is verified in the daily events of life once the self has taken on the viewpoint of faith that has been enlightened by integration.

Sometimes the intensity of enlightenment is so great that these internal events become interior *landmark* experiences. Thus, the self reaches decisive and life-directing moments that are spurred by internal religious experiences. The personal story, then, is made up not only of memorable, self-disclosing *external* happenings but, as St. Augustine points out, of internal events stimulating the inner life of man to deeper relatedness to God.

Summary

Religious growth is an ongoing organic process composed of many overlapping patterns. Like the flowing of a river there are several levels of currents, some more dominant than others at particular times in a person's life.

As individuality is encouraged, *personal appropriation* occurs as a dominating mode. Children actively participate in their own religious socialization by reaching an appreciation for certain stories, symbols, services, hymns that reflect their own unique individuality. The God-image special to each person is developed as a personal appropriation.

There is a negative side to personal appropriation, a rejection of certain less favored, unappreciated elements in one's faith tradition.

As adolescence arrives, the developed thought processes of the youngster urges mental associations and connections. What were once isolated appropriations begin to be discovered as having relationships to each other, pushing the adolescent toward the global implications of his or her faith appropriations.

There is an inclination toward commitment in the late teens or early twenties that can materialize if a dynamic role model impacts upon the life of the adolescent. Again, bonding (its own special dimension of love) is the glue that encourages the youngster to "try on" the LMS of the adult. While there may be a serious commitment to the faith tradition at this time, it is usually untested and subject to later review.

Integration is an important turning point in the life of the religiously-oriented person. It is an experience in which the personal story finds life-directing meaning in one or more aspects of the communal story, the religious heritage. Those who experience integration establish clearly for themselves what life is all about (according to the basic supposition of the Western religious tradition).

Life involves bonding to God, relating but not losing one's individuality. God is conceived under a favored image that is often carried over from the period of personal appropriation. God and man are engaged in an enterprise, the specific nature of which is determined by events from the personal story joined to an appropriated story from the communal heritage.

Integration is a religious development of the first magnitude. It may have internal "landmark" significance if it occurs as a single conversion experience. More normally, like the stream, it is part of a flowing pattern that arrives in the life of the seriously religious person over a period of time. Time is required to know the self, to log enough experience and to learn the religious heritage sufficiently to discover what truly speaks to the self.

Once integration enters into religious experience the LMS has a clearer grasp of its direction and can actively modulate all the other human systems. Of course, integration admits of degrees of intensity. It is this intensity that determines to what extent the LMS can actually motivate every aspect of the person's life. We have seen how the lives of Malcolm X and of St. Augustine were completely turned around once a high degree of integration was reached in the conversion experience.

Reappropriation is an ongoing religious experience. It is a pattern in the flow of religious growth that seems to be fortified by the enlightenments of integration. *Reappropriation* is a second level of absorption of symbol and myth. The individual thereby continues to draw rich meaning from the traditional stories and symbols of his or her faith tradition.

The same stories, symbols, and practices actually reveal new meanings as the person reflects, participates and mines from them the depth of riches that they hold. The religious journey in a way is cyclic, the participant engaging in a kind of inner pilgrimage that treads familiar ground but reaps new riches with each passing. Internal "landmark" experiences can still occur along the path, opening the self to new disclosures of a decisive kind about man's relationship and love of God.

While my stress has been on the active participation of the individual in his or her own religious growth, this is not the sole factor in the process. It is, however, the factor of growth that submits to some analysis. The other dimension is the divine ingredient, present as grace, at each level of progress in the stream, yet clearly inscrutable to human analysis.

Notes

1. James Fowler, *Stages of Faith* (San Francisco: Harper & Row, 1981), inspired by Jean Piaget, Erik Erikson and Lawrence Kohlberg, discerns six distinct stages of growth in faith. While this work contains many valuable insights, my perception is that the person of faith does not experience growth in invariant, progressive, discernible steps but in subtle, organic, transitions

that are extremely difficult to measure. I am uncomfortable with a numerical designation for a stage position so that a person is cataloged as "being in stage 4-5" of faith growth.

2. James Fowler, *ibid.*, describes some of these characteristics as part of his stage 4 category in which people begin to make strongly autonomous decisions, take up a cause, possibly break with former patterns of socialization. We observe similar phenomena and place them into differing frameworks.

BUILDING MEANING: A
THEOLOGIAN'S STORY

Chapter Eight

A critical challenge facing many adults in the Western religions, particularly Christianity and Judaism in Europe and North America, is the task of preserving the bonding to their faith traditions while accepting contemporary understandings of the world of nature and of people's relation to it, as informed by the natural and social sciences.

While discarding the earlier immature conceptualizations of the divine and of divine activity in the world they want to preserve the basic affiliative ties to God, who remains for them essential to the happenings of daily life.

The contemporary theologian faces the challenge professionally as well as personally. As educated persons theologians must address the "God question" in the context of correct scientific understanding yet preserve essential continuity with their faith tradition.

As private individuals theologians must enter the search for meaning, like the rest of us, through their own personal history of faith contending with the historical circumstances of their birth, the process of religious socialization and the personality traits given to them. Unfortunately, not many theologians share with us the elements in the personal journey that help to formulate the professional conclusions they espouse.

One theologian who does is Paul Tillich. He does not give us full entry into his private life but he does tell us what early influences helped to shape his theological thinking. This is an invaluable help in our study because Paul Tillich changed his early God-image dramatically and he also changed the dominant story-myth that formed the center of his meaning system.

In taking Tillich as a subject of investigation I do not thereby endorse his final God-image or the ethical style of his life. I find him a fascinating subject because he spends his entire life pursuing the "God question," bringing to its quest the rich resources of his strong and cultivated intellect. He finally arrives at a "God beyond God," a divinity understood as the "Ground of Being." This conceptualization is far removed from his childhood image, replacing the notion of God as a personal being with one that contemplates God as Being itself.

There is some irony, not without its humorous side, in using Tillich's book *My Search for Absolutes*[1] as a primary source for our information about him. The reason is this: the first chapter "What Am I?" supplies us with important autobiographical information indicating what Tillich thinks of himself. Given the opportunity to write approximately fifty pages about himself, he selects the material, I assume, that he considers the most valid representation of who he is. It turned out, in fact, that this was the last of his books, written just before his death.

The rest of Tillich's book is an effort to discern a pattern of absolutes first within human knowledge and then within religion. From the outset he tells us that he is bothered by the relativism of the notion of models in science as in everything else. It is as though people no longer think they can get at truth, but only close to it through models. The irony lies in using a book that searches for absolutes to uncover changing images of the divine in Tillich's own personal life!

I do not feel too badly about this because I think that Tillich's book and, I hope, my brief analysis of the evolution of his God-image use a similar methodology. In *My Search for Absolutes* Tillich's starting point is not from above, that is, not from a concept of an absolute Being about whom deductions are then made. It is from below, from a study of the structures of the human mind, from language, from the social and political strata, and of course, as typical of him, from the aesthetic.

I use a similar approach, beginning with the experiences of individual people, in order to arrive at general conclusions about life meaning. Tillich summarizes his method quite clearly for us: " . . . we have shown by analytic description the presence of absolutes within the uni-

verse of relativities and have pointed to the ground of everything absolute—the Absolute itself."[2] Therefore, he acknowledges a world filled
with relativities, and from these he proceeds with careful logic to discover the Absolute, the Ground of Being underlying and interpenetrating all relativities. His thought, while dialectic, rigorously guards
itself against self-contradiction. We might say here as a prelude to our
further study that this thinking reflects the story of Tillich's life. It is a
story that accepts a *now* God in his childhood, then is confronted with
a world overturned by a chaos of relativities. Two world wars and a
cultural revolution engulf him, yet he courageously clings to a divine
Absolute, all the while processing the inflooding relativities, not as
threats but as challenges.

The value of Tillich's theology, from my point of view, is that it
is a self-conscious effort to incorporate into a theological system the
experiences of a lifetime, careful always to preserve logical consistency,
to order this experience and to relate it to a single center. Again, the
process works from the bottom up, from man to God, rather than theoretically from the top down, from theological statements about God
to conclusions for man.

In studying man Tillich unhesitatingly draws from the social sciences and melds these findings into his theological reflections. Char-
acteristically, he says, "I do not think it is possible today to elaborate a
Christian doctrine of man, and especially a Christian doctrine of the
Christian man, without using the immense material brought forth by
depth psychology."[3]

A brief note about the subjective elements in my own research is
appropriate in studying Tillich. My study represents a certain subjective stress within the ongoing dialogue between the subjective and the
objective. Our attention has been concentrated on individual lives,
thereby sensitizing us to the fact that people see God differently at
different times in their lives. The science of human anatomy tells aspir-
ing doctors that all bodies are alike but it is quick to modify this by
adding that very few bodies are identically the same. Language would
break down, of course, if people did not have the same general awareness of the meaning of the word "God." Yet within the spectrum of
this awareness there are significant differences. Our emphasis has been
on the "significant" part of the differences.

Tillich uses the example of a red object to show the structure of the human mind, its ability to form universals. People all know the meaning of red even though they do not perceive the very same red object. I, of course, do not dispute that. But I add the affective process, even to the idea of universals, as a factor to take into consideration. Even though we all know what red is, some of us *like* red, others do not. In addition to perceiving it we have a *feeling* toward or against the color. People have favorite colors.

In other words, we stress that within the range of accepted structures of the mind, structures of language, structures of culture, there remains a latitude of *significant* diversity. This diversity often reflects the non-cognitive, affective dimension of our unique selfhood.

That is not to deny a reality "out there," whether it is a red chair, or another person, or God, all of whom we perceive out of the uniqueness of our own selfhood. The subjectivity of our unique perception does not *prevent* us from apprehending "reality." It is our indispensable aid. The diversity in religious art throughout the history of man reflects the subjectivity of individual God-images, yet at the same time this diversity contributes to the treasury of man's creativity.

Just as one learns the structure of language, that is, what everybody calls red, by a process of socialization, so one learns what others call God by the very same process. We need people to tell us what is red; we need people to tell us what is God. One is either taught a particular language system, or one is not. By the same token one is either taught a functional God dimension to reality, a *now* God, or one is not.

Therefore, while our attention is directed toward the subjective and relative aspects of human life, I assume the objective. I also assume that there is a generally similar approach among people in the West and in the East to this "objective reality" which is experienced within a similar range and understood within a commonly accepted spectrum of meanings. Each of us subjectively appropriates meanings for ourselves out of the established range of meanings taught to us by others.

Back now to Paul Tillich. In reporting on his childhood he is quick to remind us that part of his life belonged to the nineteenth century because he arrived at maturity before World War I. "I am one of those of my generation who, in spite of the radicalism with which they have criticized the nineteenth century, often feel a longing for its stability, its liberalism, its unbroken cultural traditions."[4]

How was this stability, this cultural continuity first impressed upon the youthful Tillich? The physical environment, he says, of the small medieval town in which he grew up, surrounded by a wall and centered by his father's Gothic church with its Lutheran school, gave him an experiential feeling of deep continuity with the past. Every stone stood as a witness to the history of the past "not as a matter of knowledge but as a living reality in which the past participates in the present."[5] Remarkably, he says of this setting, in which his home was almost co-extensive with the church, that it was here that he first experienced the sense of the holy. "It is the experience of the 'holy' which was given to me at that time as an indestructible good and as the foundation of all my religious and theological work."[6]

Here was the "symbolic acceptance" of his formative, childhood years. Home and church were fused; the symbols of one flowed into the other.

At the same time, the Lutheran tradition was being given to him through a deep bonding with his parents, particularly with his mother. He refers to her as less authoritarian than his father but "deeply influenced by the rigid morals of Western Reformed Protestantism."[7]

Both parents impacted on his life in their unique ways. Tillich's father, I think, set the stage, in a negative way, for his son's search for a new God-image. Tillich describes his father as a "conscientious, very dignified, completely convinced and, in the presence of doubt, angry supporter of the conservative Lutheran point of view."[8]

This strong, authoritarian example of Christian faith served as a kind of negative role model. Although bonded by deep affectionate ties to his parents he also felt very deeply confined and controlled. He says of these early influences: "The consequence was a restrictive pressure in thought as well as in action, in spite (and partly because) of a warm atmosphere of loving care. Every attempt to break through was prevented by the unavoidable guilt consciousness produced by identification of the parental with the divine authority."[9]

Symbolic acceptance led Tillich to a frame of mind in which divine and human authority were identified.

The reference to the "attempt to break through" indicates the nature of his *personal appropriation*. Tillich began his confrontation with the God-image he received in *symbolic acceptance* by confrontations with his father. This nurtured the onflowing wave of personal appropriation which had a negative cast to it. His father permitted discussion in philosophical areas, and here Tillich could safely voice his own opinions and cultivate his individuality.

Personal appropriation meant, for Tillich, among other things, fighting a Prussian father to break through to his own autonomy, his own ideas, his own individuality. Years later, Karl Barth told him he was "still fighting against the Grand Inquisitor."[10]

On the positive side Tillich appropriated the "Infra Lutheranum" doctrine of his faith, the experience of the infinite in the finite. This stayed with him his whole life, giving religious meaning to his aesthetic experiences. God was not distinctly separate from his creation, but just as the two natures of Christ were fused, so God can be discovered in creation.

Tillich loved the expansiveness of the Baltic Sea. Not only was it a communication of freedom, it was also a way of appreciating the "infinite in the finite."

Tillich, from later childhood, throughout adolescence and into his adult years, was enthralled by a sensate awareness of the infinite in the ordinary experiences of his life. He said that even the bustling city of Berlin gave him a feeling of freedom, of openness and of infinity.[11]

So the pattern began to emerge. While Tillich enjoyed many "memorable instances of 'mystical participation'" through nature he was also bothered by the demanding and authoritative God-image that had been communicated to him through the symbolic acceptance period of his childhood. He was pulled toward a kind of mystic participation of the divine in nature and he was repelled by the image of God as a demanding and unyielding father.

As this internal struggle was taking shape within him the worst possible tragedy occurred. His mother, to whom he was deeply bonded, died. This, as I indicated earlier, is the severing of the strongest human tie, the relationship to the favored parent. Consequently, the developing meaning system is devastated.

Tillich does not discuss his mother's death in *My Search for Absolutes*. His two biographers and close friends, however, tell us that her loss was quite significant in his life.[12] Rollo May, the psychologist and long-time friend, says that it was for Tillich "the most formative event up to that time, and in some ways of all his life."[13] From this shattering experience Tillich was plunged into a life of shocking relativities. There were first the new currents of philosophical and theological thought. But far more significant were the horrors of World War I which he witnessed first hand in the trenches as a chaplain. Twice he was hospitalized from emotional exhaustion. He saw his stable, secure world collapse around him. While away at war his wife was lured away from him by a personal friend. His first child died in infancy.

This convulsive sea of change that threatened to engulf his once tranquil life forced Tillich to search for an absolute underlying it all. Sometime during his duty in the trenches he finally let go of the traditional notion of God.[14] He became convinced that prayer to a personal God would not save the lives of his comrades who were being killed and maimed all around him. Camping in a forest in France he read Nietzsche's *Thus Spake Zarathustra*. The poem was an enlightenment for him, celebrating the reality of existence. It seemed to turn his thinking around. He was thirty years old at the time.

All the while Tillich had to cope with successive waves of guilt. He felt guilt about the break-up of his marriage. He felt guilt over the new freedom he discovered during his military leaves and the women with whom he became involved. He even felt the guilt of the survivor, the one who lived through the worst battles of the war, while others who were close friends paid with their lives. This sense of guilt plagued him his whole life through. It was the other side of freedom, part of the ambiguity of life that he experienced from his student days.

In an essay that Tillich wrote reflectively many years later he said that two facts appeared to him "in hours of retrospection as the all-determining facts of our life: the abounding of sin and the greater abounding of grace."[15]

This is the material of which his life-meaning synthesis was constructed. Sin, "the great all pervading problem of our life," was viewed as separation. "We are isolated, out of harmony, out of contact with all things, with each other and with nature."[16]

This tragic condition of man is neutralized by grace which binds us to the *Ground of Being* in which all share. The Ground of Being is the common bond *par excellence*. "Grace changes guilt into confidence and courage."[17]

How is this imaged in Tillich's mind? The ambiguities of life are centered and clarified by his perception of "what is happening." What is happening is that he, and people in general, are isolated and fragmented, separated from each other and even from their true selves.

They know of the sufferings of others but fundamentally are only concerned about themselves in spite of gestures of commiseration. This separation is isolation, sin. All share in it.

Yet, the absolute reality, Being itself, is the final common meeting ground, the base in which all who exist are sharers. To know of this bonding is to know absolute acceptance. Tillich envisions a voice out of the darkness and confusion of life saying, "You are accepted. You are accepted, accepted by that which is greater than you, and the name of which you do not know. Do not ask for the name now; perhaps later you will do much. Do not seek for anything; do not perform anything; do not intend anything. *Simply accept the fact that you are accepted.*"[18]

Here I submit is the core of Tillich's meaning system, the central mythology that gives meaning to all other meanings. It is the point of *integration* for him. In spite of his condition of sinfulness, his separation, his essential aloneness in life, he is accepted by the most basic, fundamental reality, Being itself. Thus there is a bonding that joins him to all else. He is not isolated: he is accepted.

The Ground of Being as an image of the divine is a God beyond the God of theism, who is neither subject nor object. Reflecting on the prayer life of those who might accept this view of the divine, Tillich reveals where he himself stands as far as prayer is concerned: "They are aware of the paradoxical character of every prayer, of speaking to somebody to whom you cannot speak because he is not 'somebody,' of asking somebody of whom you cannot ask anything because he gives or gives not before you ask, of saying 'thou' to somebody who is nearer to the I than the I is to itself. Each of these paradoxes drives the religious consciousness toward a God above the God of theism."[19]

God for Tillich, as revealed in his prayer, is beyond the framework of traditional theism. God is not a "somebody" out there. He is not a being beside other beings no matter how exalted. That kind of being is "either an object being treated as such by men or he is a subject treating men as objects."[20]

This latter designation is particularly repugnant to him, I suggest, on the balance of his home experiences and his experiences with Nazism. He says of this view of God: "God appears as the invincible tyrant, the being in contrast with whom all other beings are without freedom and subjectivity. He is equated with the recent tyrants who, with the help of terror, try to transform everything into a mere object, a thing among things, a cog in the machine they control."[21] That is the God-image he learned in his youth. It is the God-image he totally rejects in adulthood. Tillich's "new" God is above theism, "present although hidden in every divine-human encounter."[22]

Tillich has thereby come from a "totalitarian God" of childhood, surely a *now* God, to a presence with whom communion is still possible, but a presence that does not demean man or rob him of his individuality. He was able to reject the authoritarian God, while maintaining some kind of relationship with the divine as he strove to throw off guilt in the process of "freeing himself."

The caring others in his 'life, his father and mother, gave him his authoritarian God. Nature gave him his drive toward freedom, nature perceived through the unique subjective sensitivities genetically bestowed upon him. One cannot analyze Paul Tillich's God image without taking into account this unique perceptual modality. The picture we get, then, is of a childhood in which restraint is impressed upon Tillich, intellectually, religiously and environmentally. As he develops into young adulthood the normal drives to be free of parental influence are heightened by the fine-tuned perceptual sensitivities of the emerging scholar. The aesthetic experiences made possible by these sensitivities coupled with the liberalized thought of intellectual circles in pre-World War I Germany prepared him for a freeing breakthrough of thought. Finally, the chaotic events of the war unhinge him from the "rigid morals of Western Reformed Protestantism." His breakthrough was at first frightening and negative. Yet, after reading Nietzsche he began a synthesis.

All the while the non-cognitive commitment to a *now* God remained with him. This pervading awareness survived primarily in the aesthetic-mystical experiences of his life. This pursuit of the "Infra Lutheranum," the search for the infinite in the experiences of the finite, consumed him. He knew, in a way like Sheila, whom I mentioned earlier, that there was something divine in human experience that attracted him enormously.[23] He had tasted it momentarily on many occasions. He was thereby challenged to formulate cognitively a conceptualization of the elusive God-reality that he sought.

The formation of Paul Tillich's *integrating* myth which was informed by a creative God-image of his own formulation was, therefore, the result of many factors. We can see in this integration many themes from his *personal story:*

1. the desire to avoid the Prussian authority figure inspired by his father;

2. the desire to experience the fullness of personal freedom;

3. the sense of affiliation to nature, bonding to the infinite that is found in the finite;

4. the Lutheran demand for absolute faith.

These themes coalesce with the communal story he inherited, in which faith is basic trust, grace overpowers guilt. Thus bonding to the Ground of Being asserts the courage to be, inspires courage over anxiety, eliminates God as an Authoritative Being but yet lets the divine continue to be.

Paul Tillich is a clear example of a person who with intellectual sophistication and self-conscious effort departs from the God-image and story-myths of his childhood. He reframes his religious inheritance in keeping with the experiences of his personal story. With his intellectual striving, he is almost a paradigm of the outcome of Western religious thinking.

Notes

1. *My Search for Absolutes* (N.Y.: Simon and Schuster, 1967) was published after Tillich's death. It is his last statement about himself and basically repeats what he previously wrote as "Autobiographical Reflections" in C.W. Kegley and R.W. Bretall (eds.), *The Theology of Paul Tillich* (N.Y.: Macmillan Company, 1952).

2. *My Search for Absolutes*, p. 27.

3. *Ibid.*, p. 50.

4. *Ibid.*, p. 24.

5. *Ibid.*, p. 27.

6. *Ibid.*, p. 28.

7. *Ibid.*, p. 32.

8. *Ibid.*, p. 31.

9. *Ibid.*, p. 32.

10. *Ibid.*, pp. 32–33.

11. *Ibid.*, p. 29.

12. Wilhelm and Marion Pauck, *Paul Tillich, His Life and Thought* (N.Y.: Harper & Row, 1976), p. 5.

13. Rollo May, *Paulus* (N.Y.: Harper & Row, 1973), p. 40.

14. Pauck, *op. cit.*, p. 52.

15. Paul Tillich, *The Shaking of the Foundations* (N.Y.: Charles Scribner's Sons, 1948), p. 153.

16. *Ibid.*, p. 154.

17. *Ibid.*, p. 156.

18. *Ibid.*, p. 162.

19. Paul Tillich, *The Courage To Be* (New Haven: Yale University Press, 1952), p. 187.

20. *Ibid.*, p. 184.

21. *Ibid.*, p. 185.

22. *Ibid.*, p. 187.

23. Cf. the story of Sheila Chapter Two. Paul Tillich's desire to be loved as described by his wife Hannah in *From Time to Time* (N.Y.: Stein and Day, 1973) may reflect his restless search for divine love in the company of the finite (the many women who attracted him).

THE CHALLENGE OF A NEW CONSCIOUSNESS

Chapter Nine

Paul Tillich worked at creating an integration of his God-image with a satisfying and credible story-myth that was able to give meaning to his life. His need to do this arose from the conditions of his personal story. Part of this personal story was the brilliant mind he possessed and the way he cultivated it professionally, in philosophy and theology.

Most of us are not equipped with the same brilliance or with the same technical philosophical background that Tillich brought to the pursuit of life meaning. Happily we do not need to be. But we are challenged to pursue our own religious integration, discover our favored God-image and then understand the way we perceive him acting in our lives. We are compelled by the new circumstances of our time to work at a religious integration that I believe was not required of previous generations.

We have a new religious task in Western culture which was not part of the agenda for people as late as two generations ago. This task, pursuing a religious integration, once only fell upon the few, those who rose above the others, those whose personal story impelled them to this integration. They often became the dynamic religious leaders of their times. Now this same challenge of integration falls upon all and religious educators must adjust their sights to this new internal task.

The pluralism of lifestyles and life-meaning systems, publicized by the new communications networks, has changed dramatically the religious conditions of modern society. There is no longer one single communal story, out there, in the marketplace. There are many.

Tillich's life is a kind of paradigm of what happened to literally millions of people in the nineteenth and twentieth centuries. Moving by choice or by force they constituted the greatest mass migration of human beings in all of history.

Uprooted from their insular communities of faith they found themselves traveling thousands of miles from the hamlets and villages of their birth to foreign cities and countries where other faiths and lifestyles brushed them at every turn.

In the old towns, all subscribed to the same basic Christian story. The meaning of life was spelled out in the art and architecture of the local church, in the public monuments, in the structures of ecclesiastical and civil authority and in the feast days, festivals and worship services. Even Jewish communities were able to thrive within tightly-knit circles, also reinforced and nourished by their communal stories, repeated in the home and the synagogue and celebrated in worship and on feast days.

The artifacts of the medieval culture that spawned these ways of living survive in the major museums of our day. Almost every implement, not only devotional, but practical as well, tells part of the communal story. Elements of the life meaning system were emblazoned on swords and candlesticks, wedding rings, pendants and goblets, tools and ploughs.

The ordinary individual in this very different world did not feel the psychic pressure to "put it all together" in order to find a personal integration. It was together already "out there." It was as if the personal religious task of integration was not necessary. The community of faith, as the insular social community to which one belonged, possessed its own integration.

This consciousness, which is still present in countless towns and villages in many cultures today, has given rise to a new consciousness in most of the cities of the Western world.

The grandchildren and great-grandchildren of American immigrants, for example, are still on the move. They are looking for jobs in the Sun Belt, traversing the paths of corporate migration, even seeking the big opportunities in oil and mineral rich countries that are steeped in totally different religious cultures. Countless other people around the world are still fleeing either political or economic oppression.

These new travelers carry with them the new consciousness, born of the pluralistic experience. It is a consciousness that does not expect the symbols of one's religious heritage to be found in the marketplace. The new tools of the technological society, telephones and computer terminals, are not emblazoned with the symbols of any religious meaning system. The social environment is not expected to speak with a single voice about life-meaning.

This new consciousness is still unknown to literally millions of people in this world who have grown to maturity within a few miles of the place in which they were born. Their communal story remains the same as that of the many who live in the same environment with them.

But in the world of travel and instant communication the picture is very different. The individual is often confronted with a cacophony of conflicting values and options. He or she must *look for*, separate out, the familiar values of his or her heritage amidst the many options of the marketplace. The new consciousness calls for making choices, standing on one's own, forming one's own synthesis in ways never before required of believers.

In a highly mobile and communications conscious society the meaning system has to go with the individual. It does not expect reinforcement from the social environment. Thus, the meaning system must be a secure *personal* possession, carried with one, held onto in the face of competing systems. It needs to be actively constructed, a self-conscious, positive enterprise that engages the events of life, interprets them, copes with them intellectually and emotionally.

The religious educator can have an important part in this spiritual growth if he or she is willing to become a life sharer and a faith sharer. The challenge is not tangential or peripheral but central and essential. Everyone needs others to relate to, to bond to, to respond to.

Religious educators are challenged to look upon themselves a little differently than in the past. Faced with a new task, helping others to achieve their own personal religious integration, they are challenged to look upon themselves as sharers—life sharers and faith sharers.

This new task might be conceptualized as a call to be a kind of surrogate bonder. Just as children were bonded to their parents and learned the basic elements of their lifestyle from them, so now religious educators are challenged to bond to others. They will not be sharers unless they are able to establish bonds, relate to, find an emotional tie to the other. This is a basic requirement. Putting it in Christian terms they must have a genuine love for those with whom they will presume to share. Love has to be shown, expressed, made clear.

The teacher-student model is not often satisfactory as a good bonding model as a vehicle for the kind of sharing that is required. Parent-child or friend to friend models are more productive.

The word "sharing" is chosen designedly because we are not utilizing an authoritarian model in which we see religious education as a one-way process. Religious educators are aided in faith by the very people with whom they presume to share. They are on a faith journey. They too must solidify and strengthen their life meaning system.

Bonding unites both sharers. It forms a community of faith even if the community involves only two. Something very important to the religious educator must be shared, a part of oneself, one's own meaning system, one's own treasured insights, one's own way of looking upon God.

It is important to remind ourselves, however, that we cannot truly expect the other person to become a buyer of our faith-position, of our integration. We must expose ours but we cannot expect it to become theirs. That is why bonding is so important. Bonding is real sharing. The other person can experience it. Bonding is an experiential way of duplicating the God-people relationship. We try to demonstrate it. We can explain how our integration works for us. But we expect others to achieve their own integration for themselves. We leave the rest to divine grace.

Approaches to Faith Sharing

It is time to suggest several ways in which we might approach the faith sharing process. Let us start with the realization that each person who wants to share faith must possess a most basic self-awareness. That awareness is a clear understanding of our own subjective religious meaning system.

Each of us as religious educators has to realize that the God-image that we have appropriated and the one that fits neatly into *our* integration is not everyone else's. We need to be conscious of the fact that those who listen to us come from different life situations, implying a variety of God-images and a dizzying number of favored stories and possible integrations.

If we analyze some of our classes and instructions we will realize that we often expect our listeners to buy the God-image that we treasure or to go away with the religious story-myth interpreted just as we understand it. We want to give them what is in our head, what makes us tick.

The situation is sometimes worse than that. The religious teacher may be convinced that he or she is offering the *only* word of God, the single most appropriate way to understand the divine. This is proposed as *the* authentic representation of God's will for the listener.

Such a condition, so insensitively intolerant of the other's entire life situation, cannot participate in true faith sharing. It is mental oppression, strength attempting to dominate weakness, a form of brainwashing. It is not true religious education. Religious educators must know their faith position as subjectively owned, must be alert to the frame of reference out of which they function.

The listener never buys the package of meaning we have to offer. The conditions of the other person's life color the very understanding of our words and thought patterns, bringing them in line with his or her experience. Ideally, he or she must find integration and meaning for himself or herself.

The second approach to faith sharing is an awareness of the condition of the personal story of the individuals with whom we hope to share. That can only happen if we give them the opportunity to share their story with us.

We can encourage them to share their perception of God with us, suggest the ways in which they pray or the reasons that lead them to reject prayer. We can invite them to tell us various parts of their story, parts that may share with us their image of God or parts that make them think that God does not exist at all.

When people enter into these details of their lives we will often note that they use incidents from their personal story to validate the point of view they now hold. They say things like: "I think God puts us here in this world to try us, to test us. Just look at the suffering my family has had to go through."

The personal story is the basic reference point upon which the interpretation of the communal story depends. If we read a scriptural text—for example, the story of the fall of Adam and Eve—to a group and give all the participants an opportunity to share their understanding of it with us, we will discover a wide variety of interpretations of the same material. We must realize that these interpretations have been made already in each person's mind. They are based on the unique circumstances and understandings of each individual's life.

Genuine sharing of these interpretations among the group members, including the interpretation of the religious educator, may provide new possibilities of interpretation for all in the group—including the religious educator. At least it provides an opportunity for each person to objectify and articulate what he or she thinks and believes.

This kind of self-disclosure and sharing can take place within a small group setting of people who genuinely care for each other and have some kind of bond among them. Coercion of any kind, even subtle moral suasion, to have others share should be avoided.[1]

It has been my experience that people are anxious to tell parts of their story. Sometimes they want to talk out a central fact of their life story in a one-to-one setting. It requires our time, our patience and our love but it is a genuine and very important part of religious education to facilitate this kind of sharing. Often enough the simple telling of one's story crystallizes a God-image or a favored story-myth, clarifying issues of life meaning.

That brings us to the third approach to faith sharing for religious educators. It is an encouragement to individuals to find God-related meanings in their own life. We do not find meaning for them. They find their own meanings.

In keeping with our Western religious heritage we understand that God acts in history. This is ingrained in the Judaeo-Christian tradition. If that is so, can we, and can those with whom we share, find God's activity in our personal story?

Our Western heritage sets the groundwork for the understanding that God's activity is uniquely expressed in the life of individuals. Is it possible for religious educators and their faith sharers to take this understanding with complete seriousness?

If so, then each person's story is an account of the acts of God which is there for each to read. God has actually touched them individually and speaks to them now in the current events of their lives.

It might be well for the religious educator to think about the possibility that a landmark experience in the life of an individual, like the death of one's mother, is a much more momentous event *in the life of that individual* than even the redemptive death of Christ—and also that the death of one's mother can be filled with consequences for interpreting life meaning, in a way that the crucifixion of Christ might not.

Religious educators have spent great amounts of time and effort telling and interpreting the stories within the communal religious tradition, such as the meaning of the death of Christ. Clearly we can never let go of this. But we can start the other way around—start with the personal story and tie it to the communal story. This dynamic begins closer to the self.

Starting with each one's personal story we can invite them to see the connections with their communal story, to draw meaning from what is there in the communal story, to discover how the communal story gives meaning and explanation to what they have experienced.

Obviously, in religious education with children and even adolescents, the communal story is still being established. There is a great need to tell and retell the stories of the tradition, in different ways and different settings according to the age of the young people with whom one is sharing. I will suggest the practical ways of going about this in the next chapter.

But even with children and adolescents it is extremely important to hear their story, to see how they have been appropriating the building blocks in life meaning. They too can be encouraged to share with others the insights of their lives.

In the disclosures of faith-sharing one of the usual discoveries that bothers devoted religious educators is the person who thinks of God as a metaphysical ogre, the monster of the universe. It is troublesome because it seems so far from what religious educators have themselves gleaned from their tradition as a true image of God. The impulse is to rush in to change the thinking and set the hapless prisoner free of his or her chains.

Our first response in this situation might be the understanding that such an interpretation of divine activity was not learned in the communal stories of the person's religious tradition. It was learned in some painful, perhaps crushing experience of his or her personal life. A series of setbacks or a childhood without much love or a lack of sufficient bonding has gone into the formulation of this view of God. Can we expect it to be reversed overnight?

A way to approach this situation is to help the image become more consciously clear in the mind of such persons themselves. By telling their story they make it clear to themselves how they think of God. The religious educator in this case is a sounding board, one who hears the image and repeats it to the teller. "You see God as one who has singled you out for suffering." In repeating the person's point of view you are inviting him or her to acknowledge it clearly.

If change is to occur, it will only come from within the individual. The religious educator cannot change another's God image.

If change does occur we must keep in mind God's activity, the power of divine grace, a mysterious reality that we cannot predict.[2]

God's grace seems to work in bonding environments where agapeic love is demonstrated. Here again, others will express the way they view God and the interpretations of their personal story that have led them to this awareness.

Exposure to a faith sharing group whose members can articulate their perception of God and God's activity in their lives can at least be comforting for most people possessing a negative view of God.

The open faith sharing, again, must not be oppressive and domineering, assuming that others must change and change now. Even negative views of God remain relational and display an awareness of divine interest.

Open faith sharing is an honest exchange that can be, in itself, a revelational experience. It is best undertaken in a setting that includes prayer.

If bonding problems are at the base of a negative image of God, this rupture in the foundations will have to be repaired before we can expect any great change. The person needs, almost as a pre-condition for understanding a positive notion of God, the experience of a bonding relationship in his or her life. The religious educator would be well advised to notice this lack and share in whatever means can be taken to help this person improve in possible bonding relationships.

This condition points up our fourth approach to faith sharing, a deep awareness of the limit situation. Religious educators cannot transmit their own image of God, no matter how exalted, nor their privileged integration, no matter how successful for themselves. That is because religious education, at base, is not a matter of transmitting one's own spiritual achievements to others.

It is also not simply a matter of transmitting the contents of the stories that constitute one's communal religious heritage. One can expose one's own genuine understandings, one can show full appreciation for the other person's condition, one can repeat and clarify their perceptions, one can extend the love of agape toward the other. From there on, however, each individual is alone before God and makes his or her own choices and integrations.

The religious educator can only be humbly aware of his or her role as a friend, sharer, one who travels with the other. This I suggest, is true in its own way even with children. They are perceivers of their own insights. It is spiritually unproductive to view them from positions of authority, to envision oneself as having the truth that they are required to understand. However that may hold true in other bodies of knowledge, it is not useful in helping growth in religious life meaning.

A fifth approach to faith sharing keeps the focus on life meaning in contradistinction to life adjustment. The religious educator is not primarily concerned with the psychological system but with the life meaning system, the meaning that gives meaning to all other meanings. The religious educator is not a psychological counselor.

The objective of religious education is not to produce well-balanced people, however meritorious that objective. Some of the Hebrew prophets and the Christian saints would not qualify to be listed among the ranks of the most psychologically stable. They were, however, people intensely possessed of life-meaning. The grasp of religious meaning in our life does not settle our psychological problems but it does dwarf them and set them into a new perspective.

We should not confuse the use of enlightenments from the psychological sphere as an aid to self-understanding with the establishment of a life-meaning system. Psychological theories, dealing with human development, for example, should not be permitted to go beyond the limited parameters circumscribed by a psychological system. They will not serve as architectural patterns for determining what life is all about. Religious educators must keep their focus on religious meanings.

Standing behind the five approaches I have outlined is a basic sensitivity to the notion of "otherness." Religious educators are called to an appreciation of the importance and centrality of other people's lives and experience. Here is someone else's life which is complete in itself apart from us. We intersect at a point in time. That other life has a God-history to it already, of which we had no part. God has interacted with this person in the many events of his or her life but notably in the impressive and landmark experiences that create his or her self-definition.

We have not had the same experiences. That person's experiences are not ours. He or she is the one who has experienced God and life in a unique, distinctively individual way. It is for that person to read the divine interest, the divine relatedness that is demonstrated in his or her personal story.

That person's God-image will never be drawn exclusively from the communal story of his or her religious heritage. Consequently, we can never present an image of God taken from Scripture, an image that appeals to us, and expect that the other person will accept it at face value. It will only be accepted if it uniquely appeals to the other, is part of, or at least possible within, his or her personal story.

Religious education from the point of view of content has the task of presenting the wide spectrum of images under which God has been known throughout the history of one's tradition. Each individual can find in this variety of choices a way of imaging God that is distinctively appropriate for himself or herself. Within this approach to "content" there is clearly a place for the sharing of God-images and favored story myths by those who have a strong faith in God now. The religious educator is therefore a facilitator, facilitating the sharing of God-images among people who are willing to share an important part of their deepest selves.

Summary

Religious growth is an inner pilgrimage that each person, even the child, makes on his or her own. Each is challenged to respond to the ideas and values of one's communal story, as first presented through significant others. Each is also challenged to interpret the events of one's daily life, the ordinary as well as the "impressive" and "landmark" events of one's life. Religious educators can encourage others to

see in these events and in their interpretations the primary locus of
God's activity now. All can be encouraged to discern the divine activity
in their own lives, searching out a synthesis.

The synthesis is an integration in which one determines for oneself
"what is happening in my particular life." It is the same kind of synthesis that empowered the enormous energy of St. Luke's Gospel, the
same kind of synthesis that energized the convert Augustine. Each is
called to discover it for himself or herself in keeping with one's own
talents and the powerful but mysterious action of God's grace.

Notes

1. Thomas Groome, *Christian Religious Education* (San Francisco: Harper & Row, 1980), Chapter 10, outlines a method of "shared praxis" in which
he urges a spontaneous but ordered sharing starting with human experience.
I am in fundamental agreement with this fine approach, placing my emphasis, however, on the importance of bonding and "doing faith" as important
components in the process.

2. James E. Loder, *The Transforming Moment* (San Francisco: Harper
& Row, 1981), Chapter 4, stresses the divine activity in the process of "con-
victional knowing."

A PRACTICAL APPLICATION
FOR RELIGIOUS
EDUCATION

Chapter Ten

As I have outlined it, the task of the religious educator becomes one of assisting and sharing so that each individual ultimately experiences an integration in his or her life, discovers the reality of a "now" God.

The self has become known through an intimate awareness of the personal story. Similarly God has been discovered under the favored image as truly functional in one's own life story.

When God is discovered as truly relational to the self, as part of one's life and as acting fundamentally and essentially in one's behalf, then a person's LMS is centered in a religious reality. Then the meaning that gives meaning to all meanings is firmly established.

The person who has found integration has clinched the central meaning in his or her own life. The puzzle is not completely clear, however, nor is there some kind of rational synthesis that supplies all the answers to life's questions. That is not at all the case.

I do not see integration as Erikson might see an individual successfully negotiating the required psychosocial challenges of a particular age category. Neither do I see it as Jung sees the process of individuation, a kind of total adjustment of the self in a religious context so that the divinity assumes the center of the self-structure.

As I would see it, a person who is religiously integrated might still be described by others as maladjusted. I am thinking of a contemporary analyst watching the prophet Jeremiah marching around town with an oxen yoke across his shoulders or watching Francis of Assisi stripping off his fashionable clothes to become the little poor man.

Integration is rather an experiential condition that gives a basic cast and assurance to the LMS that one's basic purpose in life is straight. As I know who I am, I know who God is, in relation to me. Priorities are set by this and one can live life according to this awareness.

Integration is not only for saints and prophets, though, as I have said, saints and prophets experienced it. Integration is for all ordinary people who can discover in their communal story the unique meaning that speaks to them personally about God in their lives.

It has been my point that religious integration is never achieved in total isolation from others. These others (even if it be only one other person) provide the bonding that is absolutely essential in everyone's life as a prerequisite to achieving integration. Without bonding, people are unable to discover the basic experience of relationality upon which Western religious experience is based.

The ideal in the Western religious framework, relating to God and responding to God's relationship, must be actualized in life experience at the human level to be fully appreciated as the authentic arena of divine activity.

If this is true it follows that the enormous educational efforts that are directed solely toward children by the various religious groups might be ready for a major change. If bonding is really what is at issue in a very fundamental way, then adults as well as children ought to enter into the religious educational process. Children will be aided in their faith through bonding to the adults who are able to achieve a religious integration in their own lives.

Two issues, then, emerge as important to religious educators. The first is the importance of bonding and the threats to bonding that are posed in the lives of individuals. The second is the need for integration on the part of many adults and the kind of assistance that can be given to aid in its accomplishment.

We have already identified the bonding problems in people's lives. In American society the number one problem is the broken family. It can be broken by death, divorce, alcoholism or drugs.

It stands to reason that religious bodies will have to place the highest priority on helping the families and the individuals whose meaning systems have been endangered or devastated by these causes. This means that an approach to religious education taken by religious bodies must be intensely personal and individual.

Under the present system in churches and synagogues the personal element is not fostered. Children come for religious instruction and the teacher exchanges niceties with the parent who drops off and picks up the child. It is as if the child were an isolated entity. It is a kind of unintended conspiracy of sorts in which the child is in the middle, the one who cannot object to what is happening. Parents keep their values to themselves; teachers keep their values to themselves. The child, as a subject for instruction, is somewhere in the middle.

Parents have the essential and final responsibility for the religious education of their children. In a real sense it is impossible to delegate this responsibility to an outside professional. Parents are unable to delegate their bonding relationship. Similarly, they cannot delegate their God image (or lack thereof) to a religious professional. The task of religious education lies with them, and if they have not achieved an integration in their own lives the task will not be accomplished satisfactorily.

This means that parents will have to find their own ways of fostering prayer in the home, explaining the story-myths of their faith, and instructing their children in the proper ways of participating in community worship.

If we take an example from the Roman Catholic tradition, parents will have to assume the responsibility of determining when their children are ready for their first experience of the sacraments. They will also have to assume responsibility for preparing them for the sacraments. These responsibilities formerly resided with the pastor and his professional helpers. The help from professionals will now come in the form of assistance *for parents*. The helping link in religious education will be between the parents and the professional in order to accomplish the essential task which is between the parent and the child.

It is in working with broken "households," households affected by death, divorce, alcoholism or abandonment, that religious educators must bring new skills. These circumstances require sensitive and well prepared professionals with new competencies in counseling skills, and family dynamics in addition to their basic religious grounding. The knowledge of counseling skills is not for the purpose of aiding in the readjustment of a maladjusted family. Religious education has not become counseling.

These skills are put to specifically religious purposes such as trying to identify with parents how their own meaning systems have been affected and the meaning systems of the children have been jolted by the tragedies that beset the family.

There will be a need to work one-on-one or in small groups to determine ways in which meaning can be reconstructed. In this capacity the religious educator is a faith sharer, a facilitator, a bonder and a participator with the other adults present.

The religious educator can help people understand their favored God image and how that image can be functional in the present circumstances. In cases where the God-image is unsatisfying the person can be aided in an awareness of its inadequacies, assisted in viewing God differently.

As I have been insistent in stressing throughout this book each adult must find a "now" God for himself or herself, an image of God that is appropriate for discovering the activity of God in his or her everyday life. Once that can be accomplished a major task in religious education is achieved. The religious professional can provide help in this area.

It is also part of the work of the religious professional to be a facilitator, to bring adults together. This is no small, incidental task. It is a major accomplishment when it happens. Once together, minimal levels of trust can be established so that some genuine sharing takes place.

In these small learning-sharing sessions the "content" is drawn from the favored story myths that are suggested by the participants themselves. The religious educator listens attentively to the explanations of the stories that each adult favors because in them are bound up the key to a present or a future integration.[1]

The adults are asked whether this story appeals to some aspect of their life that they might be willing to share. In this beginning and tentative way each person is encouraged to identify a favored communal story and an impressive or landmark event in his or her life.

Through this means, each individual stays with the concrete events of his or her own personal life. They all learn to look into their own life to discover God acting in their own personal history. They all begin to understand their personal story as an account of God's action in history and learn to interpret the events of their individual lives as the central event of God's "now" activity.

Prayer, even if it is brief, is an essential part of these sessions. It is the basic way of continuing the relationship with a "now" God. Each person has the opportunity to formulate a prayer, making explicit the way he or she thinks about God. Adults begin to become familiar with themselves praying aloud. This kind of prayer is very much "confessional," that is, in a gentle way it professes one's belief in God or one's willingness to believe. Prayer is also an aid to bonding, helping to join this small group together. The prayers stand alone; they are never subjected to any kind of analysis in this setting. Personal prayer is also encouraged, and here again spontaneity is recommended.

With the emphasis on adults, the question may be asked, "Do you mean to let go completely of the religious education of children as it is conducted under religious auspices?" I do not. But I emphasize that this be acknowledged as clearly supplemental. It is not "business as usual" except that we pay greater attention to the adults. It is that religious education is *centrally concerned* with adults and what is done with children flows from that.

All adult religious education needs to have the practical dimension of "doing faith," that is, learning and sharing, in order to be of service to others. "Doing faith" for the adults who are part of these small groups can mean serving as the nucleus for those who work with children.

There are other communities "out there" besides the home that children relate to. The school is one. The church can be another. Religious education can go on under the auspices of a church community. I suggest, however, that this religious education be built on the "home model." I suggest it not take place in the church building but in private homes.

In the home setting, children associate with several of their peers and with a parent model, concentrating on learning and "doing" their faith. They come to understand that children of the same faith think somewhat differently but there is a bonding unity that brings them together in a kind of family atmosphere.

Here is an occasion to be away from one's own parents but to be with a parent model. The adult who is working with these groups tries to establish a rapport that functions similar to a healthy parent-child relationship. For the adult conducting these sessions this calls for a conscious effort at identifying the self as a kind of surrogate parent, one who is helping the child toward religious maturity.

The teacher-pupil model is not an effective model for faith sharing. When religious educators conceive of themselves as teachers before a class they tend to mask feelings, think in terms of delivering content, and become concerned with proper discipline. None of these attitudes facilitates bonding. Conducting religious education in a classroom environment contributes heavily toward fostering the teacher-pupil model. The home environment is much better for translating out as a bonding environment.

Each religious educator, in order to function in a parent role, cannot be responsible for too many children. As the number of children increases the classroom model gains re-entry. Five or six children for each teacher will preserve the model beautifully.

This may seem unreal, particularly in parishes where large numbers of children are involved in religious instruction. But the "problem" of large numbers absolutely must be dealt with because large groups automatically change the model in themselves and defeat the true purpose of religious education. Crucial to religious education is the preservation of the parent model.

To be very practical, I suggest that parents who are sufficiently interested in their children receiving religious education under organizational auspices be enlisted to participate as volunteers to the degree they find it possible. Allowing for those parents who feel totally incapable of doing this or who are prevented from participating for other reasons, the body of religious educators should be drawn from the homes of adults who care about the religious education of children. They will need both assistance and assurance from professional parish coordinators and organizers, but that assistance, at another level, will constitute their own participation in the faith-sharing process.

Trying to build a bonding relationship with other people's children is not easy. A certain barrier needs to be broken through with these other parents. The parents need to get together to talk about the needs and interests of the child. This kind of personal attention and communication is only possible with small groups. The interaction at the present level is healthy and opens up the possibility of building adult relationships, but it requires a certain amount of facilitation from third persons acting as coordinators.

The beginning of a religious education program, or its revision, calls for starting with small groups of adults, assisted by a religious professional. Only after these groups are organized and functioning as aids to integration and reappropriation should the parish begin to organize the children.

Those adults who have expressed a willingness to share their faith with others and to become involved in "doing faith" can be the first to participate in the religious education of children.

Children of Primary Grade Age

What do we do with small groups of children once we have them? I will treat of what might happen in these groups from two perspectives, but they are simply that—perspectives. They are two dimensions of the very same process, an emotional dimension and an intellectual dimension. First, we will talk about the emotional dimension.

Giving and receiving, making and sharing together are the means toward establishing a bonding relationship. Children at this age want to participate with others and with the religious educator in making things for others, in giving to others, and, very importantly, in getting something for themselves.

Whatever participatory activities can be devised to interrelate children, one to the other, will help a sense of relatedness. Each session ought to have a "doing faith" aspect to it in which the children understand that their religious tradition is synonymous with doing something for others. This can be an "acting out" of a drama or a real situation in which every child gets a chance to participate.

Prayer, either sung or verbal, is an important part of each session even if it is brief. Prayer establishes a relational bond with God within this human relational setting. Encouraging children to formulate their own prayers leads them to articulate their view of God. Again, religious educators are participants, not directors or teachers. They take their turn like the rest and their prayer unassumingly serves as a model.

From the intellectual point of view the task is to feed their imaginations with the stories of the community tradition. The "content" consists in reading and telling the stories of Scripture and of the tradition. The heroic and responsive deeds of prophets and saints are beautifully appropriate.

It is my suggestion that throughout the religious education of children (until adolescence) the content focus on stories that involve the exploits and relationships of *people*. It really does not matter how long ago these people lived if their stories can be understood by the children. I emphasize "people" in contradistinction to "ideas" like "building community" or "the community in which I live," even "the Eucharist as a sign of God's love."

It is not even necessary to have stories form an idea "unit" such as "faith" in which the educator brings together all the heroes of faith. That is to make the mistake of imposing an adult organizing principle upon the material.

Children will begin to synthesize in their own good time. They will put the mosaic together for themselves when the time is personally ripe for them. The most important consideration is that they learn the stories of their faith as "insiders," as belongers in exactly the same way they learned language. The heroes in these stories are in some way related to them, part of their heritage, members of their religious family.

Children at Intermediate Grade Age Level

Children at the ages of nine, ten and eleven are in a perfect age to enjoy bonding. They are anxious to associate with each other but often are at a loss to know how to do it except with one or two close friends.

Functioning out of the parent model, the religious educator can build on this natural tendency. The world is wider for these children and they can get out into it with more security than their younger brothers and sisters. Trips together are invaluable aids to bonding. Furthermore, trips to cathedrals, museums, nursing homes, etc., relate them to the real world in their religious experience.

In their small groups they learn the family religious experience, that is, that what brings them together is their membership in the same faith tradition. Prayer together binds them and their prayer is often directed toward the successful accomplishments of their "doing faith" projects.

Intellectually, new strides are taken. Since their reading abilities have matured beyond beginning stages it is time to let them choose their own religious biographies and Bible books. Here again, the instructional model should not inveigle itself into the group sessions. Book reports are not necessary. Formal presentations of material covered are not necessary. What is important is that each child learn to share his or her honest feelings about what he or she has read.

If the religious educator uses filmstrips to stimulate discussion the important part of each session is the children's willingness and ability to speak their mind and their feelings. An individual response, not pressured by the adult present, but welcomed as the children's input into the meaning of faith for them, is the ideal of participation. There is no "ground" to be covered even though there is much intellectual "content" for each child.

"Doing faith" is essential to the religious education process. That cannot be stressed too often. Involvement in an activity that will benefit others needs to be planned and worked out by the group as an ordinary and expected outcome of their being together.

Bonding in the Early Teens

When children reach the ages of twelve, thirteen and fourteen the parent model needs to be supplemented with another model which relates to the family setting. It might be called "the big brother, big sister model."

Youngsters in this age category need living models, closer in age to themselves, to *supplement* the parent-like presence. Eighteen or nineteen year olds are a perfect addition to the group to share themselves along with the adult present. This is also the way that older teenagers will receive their religious education. It can be the "doing faith" aspect of their own religious growth. There is a vitality and cross-fertilization in this kind of arrangement, the older teenager feeling responsible for working with and sharing with others, the younger ones looking up to an older model who is willing to give time and attention to them.

The intellectual and "content" perspective of religious education can be developed during these years without introducing the school model. Youngsters "study" all kinds of things on their own outside of school, from cooking and computers to drawing and driving. In the religious education setting they can be encouraged to select a project for study that they can explain to the other members of the group and that can lead to some form of "doing faith." They select the topic, receive help from the adult and older teenager when necessary, and share their findings with the group when they are finished. This approach can utilize a more serious and organized approach to contemporary issues, moral questions, Scripture study and the study of one's faith tradition.

There can be solid "content" here which the youngsters generate and share with all so that even the religious educator can learn something.

The entire objective is to avoid two eminently prevalent approaches. One starts with the religious educator who has a pre-packaged curriculum, formulated by experts, in the form of a textbook. However garishly illustrated, it is still a text proposing a series of topics that may or may not correspond with the mental and emotional framework of the students. "Teachers" then prepare their "lesson" from this text to present to the children. The greatest benefit in this approach comes to the "teacher" who selects the ideas according to his or her God image, favored stories and unique integration. The children may be in an entirely different frame of reference.

Another current method employs a brief preliminary presentation and then invites the youngsters for their comments about it. This is better insofar as it evokes some kind of response from the children, but it does not involve them heavily enough in their own planning. They become simply commentators on someone else's work.

Starting with the position we have been espousing—that the nature of the times in which we live requires each person to develop one's own religious stance and generate one's own life meaning system—the child should rather be introduced to the religious quest as young as possible. The process can and should have sound intellectual content to it. It should arise out of the interest and the meanings that the child is able to perceive.

The adult with the group and the older teenager become resource people who, knowing the children personally, can react to their initiatives and suggest ways of studying and courses of action. Here is a small cell unit in which children learn to respect each other's interests, to listen to the topics they have chosen to study and to be influenced by the thoughts and convictions of others who are part of their group.

Prayer together has the effect of bonding them to each other before God, giving them a sense of being together in something very important to each of them. Each member of the group, and the religious educator as well, ought to formulate a personal prayer that can be shared with the others. This further helps to articulate a view of God, positioning oneself, taking a stand about how one views God and what one expects of the divine-human relationship.

Bonding for Older Teens

Bonding is built through the exchange of ideas and feelings within the context of a sharing group. For older teens the parental model serves as a kind of reference point against which new ideas are tested. The peer influence is great, but again a young adult in his or her early twenties can serve in a "big brother, big sister" capacity without alluding to it in those terms.

This is the age when religion can take on major importance and when global perspectives are beginning to be developed. While it is a very busy age, with young people working at part-time jobs, participating in athletic or musical activities, cultivating their social life and preparing for college, it is also a prime time for personal religious development. Religious educators should not neglect young people at this age level.

Small cells can be brought together consisting of five or six seventeen and eighteen year olds with an adult and a young adult in his or her twenties. Starting with what is important to their own personal religious understanding they establish what will be their individual areas of investigation. They relate this investigation to a "doing faith" project that interests them.

Alerted to what each person is working on, they remain sensitive to ideas, thoughts and material that may be useful to the others in their projects. For some, the "doing faith" projects will incorporate their work with younger children as I mentioned above, their participation in the activities of cells in another age group.

A whole world of ideas and religiously related topics is open to the group. For some groups a need to stay within one general area such as "Moral Questions" may be their discernment. In this case various individuals would study and report back on what they have learned that is of interest to them in specific moral areas. The involvement of the religious educator with each individual young person is what is essential.

For other groups the interests may vary widely. It does not really matter that there are five or six completely different religious topics discussed in a five month period. What does matter is that youngsters be held responsible (as they usually are by their peers) for accurate reporting and genuine sharing of the enlightenments they have discovered.

Summary

The very first experience of human life is the experience of graciousness, the loving care of parents. This is experienced through bonding. In the Western conceptualization this experience serves as a ground for the experience of God. God is conceptualized as a gracious One, the relater to man *par excellence*. God can be understood in this context only when man has experienced graciousness for himself.

Thus the first locus for the discovery of the meaning of God is in the personal story. Impressive events are the hills and valleys that contour meaning for us. The personal story is the individual history of God's acts in our lives.

But the personal story is given frames of reference, structures of meaning by the communal story which is imparted to us through loving bonders. It is *our group* story, a story for insiders.

It tells of a family of believers, wider than our nuclear family, whose existence verifies the communal story. Bonders from this wider community help us to see the many varied dimensions of that story which we would not know on our own through our own experience.

Thus God touches us through this second locus of divine activity, the community members. The stories of the communal tradition live on through its members who treasure its many dimensions and recognize God acting in it. The communal story sheds light on the many different meanings in the events of one's personal story.

Personal story—communal story: two foci of the ellipse that encompasses meaning for us, two pillars of the arch that cap life meaning. All are challenged to discover their own structure of meaning out of their ingredients. Each must discern, through the community's enlightenment, the divine voice that whispers in the individual moments of his or her life. Paradoxically, we are both alone and with others. We search out our own way but others walk with us. The God who becomes "now" has actually been with us all the way.

Note

1. I see the adult presentation of a favorite story as very close to what Thomas Groome, *Christian Religious Education* (San Francisco: Harper & Row, 1980), p. 207, calls "Naming the Present Action." We seem to agree on starting with the person's basic interest, having him or her articulate it, and inviting the others to respond with sensitivity.

BIBLIOGRAPHY

Allport, Gordon, *The Individual and His Religion* (New York: The Macmillan Company, 1950).

Augustine, Saint, *The Confessions of Saint Augustine* in *The Fathers of the Church*, trans. by Vernon J. Bourke (New York: Fathers of the Church, Inc. 1953).

Comeau, Sr. Irene, S. S. J., "Not Quite Ten Years Later," unpublished Master's thesis, Fairfield University, Fairfield, Connecticut, 1972.

Daly, Mary, *Beyond God the Father* (Boston: Beacon Press, 1973).

Dulles, Avery, *Models of the Church* (New York: Doubleday, 1974).

Eliade, Mircea, *The Cosmos and History* (New York: Harper Torchbook, 1959).

Erikson, Erik H., *Childhood and Society*, 2nd ed. (New York: Norton, 1963).

Fowler, James, *Stages of Faith* (San Francisco: Harper & Row, 1981).

Fowler, James and Keen, Sam, *Life-Maps: Conversations on the Journey of Life* (Waco, Texas: Word Books, 1978).

Freud, Sigmund, *The Future of an Illusion* (New York: W. W. Norton, 1961)

Furth, Hans G., *Piaget for Teachers* (Englewood Cliffs, New Jersey: Prentice-Hall, 1970).

Goldman, Ronald, *Religious Thinking from Childhood to Adolescence* (New York: Seabury, 1965).

Groome, Thomas H., *Christian Religious Education* (San Francisco: Harper & Row, 1980).

Heschel, Abraham, *The Prophets*, Vol. I (New York: Harper & Row, 1969).

Kohlberg, Lawrence, "The Child as Moral Philosopher," *Psychology Today* (September 1968).

Levinson, Daniel *et al.*, *The Seasons of a Man's Life* (New York: Knopf, 1978).

Loder, James E., *The Transforming Moment* (San Francisco: Harper & Row, 1981).

Malcolm X, *The Autobiography of Malcolm X* (New York: Grove Press, 1964).

May, Rollo, *Paulus* (New York: Harper & Row, 1973).

Niebuhr, Reinhold, *Moral Man and Immoral Society* (New York: Charles Scribner's Sons, 1932).

Pauck, Wilhelm and Pauck, Marion, *Paul Tillich, His Life and Thought* (New York: Harper & Row, 1973).

Perrin, Norman, *The Resurrection According to Matthew, Mark and Luke* (Philadelphia: Fortress, 1977).

Ramsey, Ian, *Models and Mystery* (London: Oxford University Press, 1965).

Ramsey, Ian, *Myths, Models and Paradigms* (New York: Harper & Row, 1974).

Smith, Huston, "Accents of the World's Religions," in John Bowman (ed.), *Comparative Religion* (Leiden: Brill, 1972).

Smith, Wilfred Cantwell, *The Meaning and End of Religion* (New York: Macmillan, 1963).

Tillich, Paul, *Dynamics of Faith* (New York: Harper & Row, 1977).

Tillich, Paul, *My Search for Absolutes* (New York: Simon & Schuster, 1967).

Tillich, Paul, *The Shaking of the Foundations* (New York: Charles Scribner's Sons, 1948).

Tillich Paul, *The Courage To Be* (New Haven: Yale University Press, 1952).

Tillich, Hannah, *From Time to Time* (New York: Stein and Day, 1973).

Tracy, David, *Blessed Rage for Order* (New York: Seabury, 1975).

Westerhoff, John H., *Will Our Children Have Faith?* (New York: Seabury, 1976).

Wilder, Amos Niven, *Theopoetic: Theology and the Religious Imagination* (Philadelphia: Fortress, 1976).